SOCIAL WORK
QUALITY ASSURANCE
PROGRAMS:

A COMPARATIVE ANALYSIS

SOCIAL WORK QUALITY ASSURANCE PROGRAMS:

A COMPARATIVE ANALYSIS

CLAUDIA J. COULTON, PH.D.

*Assistant Professor, School of Applied Social Sciences,
Case Western Reserve University, Cleveland, Ohio*

NATIONAL ASSOCIATION OF SOCIAL WORKERS, INC.
1425 H Street, N.W. Washington, D.C. 20005

International Standard Book No.: 0-87101-080-1
Library of Congress Catalog Card No.: 79-64941
NASW Catalog No.: CBH-080-C

Printed in the U.S.A.

3

Cover and interior design by the Wenk Organization

CONTENTS

LIST OF TABLES

FOREWORD

THIS PUBLICATION is the result of two years of work by the Committee on Health Quality Standards of the National Association of Social Workers (NASW) and the Joint Committee of NASW and the American Hospital Association (AHA). It is another step in the mutual efforts of these two organizations to encourage the development of standards for social work practice in health care. The first tangible effort was the process that led, in 1977, to the AHA publication *Development of Professional Standards Review for Hospital Social Work.* That document examined legislative and regulatory requirements for (1) utilization review, (2) peer review, and (3) audit. It proposed minimal structural standards for social work professional standards review in hospitals.

In the spring of 1977, the NASW Committee on Health Quality Standards, recognizing that quality assurance programs would be important in setting and implementing standards for social work practice in health care, undertook the task of developing a companion publication on quality assurance. Upon obtaining the approval of NASW's Board of Directors, the Health Quality Standards Committee and the NASW staff commissioned a nationwide study of social work quality assurance programs. The committee employed Claudia Coulton, then a doctoral candidate at Case Western Reserve University School of Applied Social Sciences, as a consultant. This monograph became possible because of her creativity, dedication, hard work, and magnificent ability to meet all required timetables with seeming effortlessness. The committee wishes to thank her most gratefully and with deep affection.

The committee is also indebted to the Society for Hospital Social Work Directors of the AHA for its complete cooperation in this huge study and for making resources available quickly at many points along the way. To Salie Rossen, secretary of the society, our special thanks for all her assistance, support and advice, which gave the committee the benefit of the struggle to bring into print the 1977 document on professional standards review.

During the past year and a half, the executive director of NASW, Chauncey Alexander, and the staff at the national office have contributed many hours of assistance, advice, support, and an ingenius capacity to stretch the funds allotted for the task. Mention must be made of two staff members especially important to the work of the Committee on Health Quality Standards, Glenn Allison, the former program director of NASW, and Maryanne Keenan, the staff associate to the committee. For their unstinting efforts, the committee is grateful.

My personal thanks to the past and present members of the Committee on Health Quality Standards. I am certain all share with me a sense of pride and accomplishment at having seen this important study through to completion and publication.

Members of the committee include Genevieve Carter, Tessie Cleveland, Felix Gonzalez, Bernice Harper, Thomas Holland, Benjamin Lewis, Helen Rehr, Harry Schonfeld, and Patricia Volland.

LAWRENCE C. SHULMAN, *Chairperson*
Committee on Health Quality Standards
National Association of Social Workers

April 1979

1
INTRODUCTION

IN THE PAST FEW YEARS, there has been a rapid development of quality assurance programs in the health care field. Social workers around the country have been working to develop procedures to assess and improve the quality of their services. Working independently, several regional groups and individual hospital social work departments have created, tested, and implemented quality assurance programs. The Health Quality Standards Committee of the National Association of Social Workers (NASW) wanted to make the results of these efforts available to others in the field and to establish some uniform guidelines for social work quality assurance programs. The committee therefore requested NASW to commission a study of several existing quality assurance programs. The study was undertaken in August 1977. This volume is a report of the study and its implications.

The purpose of this report is to make generally available the experience of several groups that have developed quality assurance programs. The report is not intended to recommend any one program, but to identify similarities and areas of agreement that can be used in moving toward some uniformity in quality assurance activities. The report provides examples of components of programs that are presently in use and an analysis of the characteristics of these programs. Since this analysis suggests some advantages and disadvantages of alternative approaches, it can be used to guide hospital social work departments and regional groups as they develop their own programs. The examples presented may also be modified for use elsewhere. Further, the report suggests some general quality assurance principles and identifies some issues that will require solution.

1

Chapter 2 presents some background of the quality assurance concept and recent activities of the social work profession in this area. It also discusses some of the concepts and terminology relevant to quality assurance. Chapter 3 describes the methodology used in conducting the study. Chapter 4 reports the findings of the study, comparing the programs in important areas and suggesting advantages and disadvantages of various approaches. Chapter 5 suggests some basic principles and standards for quality assurance as evidenced by the study's findings. It also identifies some issues that need to be addressed and predicts some future directions for quality assurance in social work.

Summary of Findings

Among the major findings of the study reported herein are the following:

1. Social work quality assurance programs contain one or more of the following components:

   - A patient-oriented information system.
   - A peer review system.
   - A system for assuring social work coverage.

The most complete programs contain all three components, and these are interrelated, that is, the findings from one component serve as input for the other components. Peer review is the most prevalent component.

2. Social work information systems tend to record at least the following data elements:

   - Physical and social characteristics of patients.
   - Problems or goals.
   - Services received.
   - Outcomes for patients.

These data elements are measured in a variety of ways, with the most substantial variations among programs occurring

2

around classifications of patients' problems and social interventions. The precise measurement of outcomes for patients also requires further development.

3. Social work peer review systems tend to contain criteria in the following areas:

- Initial contact.
- Assessment.
- Formulation of goals.
- Actual intervention.
- Termination/outcome.

There are striking similarities among peer review systems on many criteria in each of these areas. Systems differ, however, on other important dimensions, such as these:

- Is a single set of criteria developed for all patients, or is a separate set developed for each disease or social problem category?
- Are the actual reviews conducted by social workers or other specially trained personnel?
- Do the criteria focus on the social work process or the outcome for patients?

4. Systems to assure social work access are just beginning to emerge. They tend to contain lists of patients' characteristics that indicate a high probability that social work services will be required.

5. The monetary costs of quality assurance programs can be minimized if the following measures are adopted:

- The input forms required for the information system are simple.
- The computer program for the information system is efficient and is not written prematurely before the system stabilizes.
- The number of peer review criteria is limited and can be applied by non-social work personnel.
- The number of people incorrectly identified by the access indicators as needing service is minimized.

6. The findings of quality assurance programs are used in

- Making management decisions.
- Evaluating the performance of workers.
- Identifying the need for in-service training and continuing education.
- Guiding policy change.
- Contributing to social work knowledge.

7. Social work quality assurance programs can interface with the activities of a hospital's Peer Service Review Organization (PSRO) activities. Some examples follow:

- Social work retrospective studies based on peer review or on special analysis of information system data can serve as medical care evaluation studies.
- Access indicators can be incorporated into concurrent review criteria.
- Specific or general social work criteria can be incorporated into interdisciplinary or multidisciplinary medical care evaluation studies.
- Analysis of data from the information system can produce profile analyses.

8. The validity of many aspects of social work quality assurance programs is yet to be established. Key questions include the following:

- Do patients whose care is judged acceptable according to process criteria actually have an increased probability of positive outcomes?
- Do the classification schemes for patients' problems and social services actually produce a meaningful and reliable categorization of cases?

These and other findings are documented and discussed in the chapters that follow.

2
BACKGROUND

EFFORTS TO PROMOTE high-quality service are not new to the social work profession. Supervision in which the work of one social worker is reviewed by one who is more experienced or more highly trained constitutes a traditional attempt to raise the quality of social work practice. The training and accreditation provided in social work education programs are intended to influence the quality of practice through controlling the knowledge base of persons entering the profession. Licensing and certification require social work professionals to have certain qualifications that are believed necessary for practice of an acceptable quality. Moreover, structural standards for social work practice in health care have existed for some time and are regularly revised to reflect the developments in the field.[1] These standards have been created specifically to insure quality.

Recently, some additional approaches for promoting high-quality service have emerged. These approaches have been broadly referred to as quality assurance programs. They include some new methodologies and consist of activities designed to examine systematically the quality of care actually delivered to patients and to correct any observed deficiencies. The more recently developed quality assurance programs are the focus of this report.

---

[1] See, for example, Joint Committee of the American Hospital Association and the National Association of Social Workers, *Standards for Hospital Social Services* (Washington, D.C.: National Association of Social Workers, 1976); and Social Work Section, American Public Health Association, "Educational and Experience Qualifications for Social Workers in Health and Medical Care Programs" (Washington, D.C.: American Public Health Association, 1977).

Mandates for Quality Assurance

Many factors have led to social work's present level of interest in systematic quality assurance programs that are focused on the care of patients. First, consumers of all types are demanding that providers of goods and services be accountable for their products, and social workers are desirous of meeting this demand.[2] Second, questions have been raised about whether social services actually have a positive effect on clients.[3] The profession, therefore, must build its knowledge about what interventions, under what circumstances, produce desired outcomes. Third, funds for human service programs are scarce, and those who compete for them must support their requests for funds with evidence of the quality of their services.

Fourth, in 1972, Title XI of the Social Security Act was amended as a result of Public Law 92–603. This amendment required that certain procedures be implemented so "the services for which payment may be made under the Social Security Act will conform to the appropriate professional standards for the provision of health care."[4] The guidelines for the development and implementation of such procedures appear in the *PSRO Program Manual*.[5] This manual prescribes, among other things, that nonphysician health care practitioners must be involved in the review of care provided by their peers.[6] They

---

[2] *See,* for example, Emanuel Tropp, "Expectation, Performance, and Accountability," *Social Work,* 19 (March 1974), pp. 139–148; George Hoshino, "Social Services: The Problem of Accountability," *Social Service Review,* 47 (September 1973), pp. 373–383; Marvin Rosenberg and Ralph Brody, "The Threat or Challenge of Accountability," *Social Work,* 19 (May 1974), pp. 344–350; and Edward Newman and Jerry Turem, "The Crisis of Accountability," *Social Work,* 19 (January 1974), pp. 5–16.

[3] *See,* for example, Hans Eysenk, "The Effects of Psychotherapy: An Evaluation," *Journal of Consulting Psychology,* 16 (July 1952), pp. 319–324; Charles Truax and Robert Carkhuff, *Towards Effective Counseling and Psychotherapy* (Chicago: Aldine Publishing Co., 1967); Steven Segal, "Research on the Outcome of Social Work Therapeutic Intervention: A Review of the Literature," *Journal of Health and Social Behavior,* 13 (March 1972), pp. 3–17; Edward J. Mullen, James R. Dumpson, and Associates, *Evaluation of Social Intervention* (San Francisco: Jossey-Bass, 1972); Joel Fischer, "Is Casework Effective? A Review," *Social Work,* 18 (January 1973), pp. 5–21; and Fischer, *The Effectiveness of Social Casework* (Springfield, Ill.: Charles C Thomas, 1976).

[4] *Social Security Act,* Title XI, Sec. 1151.

[5] *PSRO Program Manual* (Washington, D.C.: U.S. Department of Health, Education & Welfare, February 1977).

[6] Ibid., sec. 520.08.

are to develop and apply their own norms, criteria, and standards and should work with the PSRO committee when their services are reviewed.[7] Nonphysicians are also to serve as an advisory group to PSRO.[8] Although the predominant approach to the review of ancillary services is to be through retrospective review, such practitioners should provide consultation when concurrent review reveals problems related to their area of practice.[9]

Fifth, the Joint Commission on Accreditation of Hospitals (JCAH) requires that hospitals and mental health facilities have a program to evaluate patient care and that the program evaluate the quality of the social services.[10] This is consistent with the standards for hospital social services promulgated by NASW.[11] Further, the JCAH *Accreditation Manual for Hospitals* suggests that quality of care studies be multidisciplinary.[12]

Social Work's Efforts

Several organizations and agencies have been actively engaged in studying issues in quality assurance for social work. In 1976, NASW established a committee on health quality standards to oversee PSRO policy and professional issues. Many state chapters have also formed committees to represent social work in PSRO activities and to begin to develop approaches to quality assurance in the social services. Since 1975, NASW has periodically distributed a PSRO newsletter to keep social workers in health care informed of the latest developments in quality assurance programs.

The Society for Hospital Social Work Directors of the American Hospital Association has been involved in the pro-

---

[7] Ibid., sec. 730.32.

[8] *Federal Register* (January 25, 1977), p. 4635.

[9] *Technical Assistance Document No. 9* (Washington, D.C.: U.S. Department of Health, Education & Welfare, January 25, 1977).

[10] *Hospital Survey Profile* (Chicago: Joint Commission on Accreditation of Hospitals, 1978), p. 145; and "Quality of Professional Services," insert to *Accreditation Manual for Psychiatric Facilities* (Chicago: Joint Commission on Accreditation of Hospitals, 1976).

[11] *Standards for Hospital Social Services* (Washington, D.C.: National Association of Social Workers, August 1977).

[12] *Accreditation Manual for Hospitals* (Chicago: Joint Commission on Accreditation of Hospitals, 1977).

motion of accountability for hospital social work departments for some time. During the last five years, it has held a conference and annual meetings on the theme of accountability. Its committees and task forces have focused on topics such as a uniform reporting system, recording in medical records, and cost accountability. It cosponsored, with NASW, a working conference on social work and PSRO issues and published a report of the proceedings.[13]

The Maternal and Child Health Services division of the Bureau of Community Health Services has sponsored a series of conferences conducted by the Public Health and Social Work programs at the University of Pittsburgh and the University of California at Berkeley. Four of these conferences have focused on quality assurance issues and programs.[14] The federal End-Stage Renal Disease Program has experimented with multidisciplinary audits that include social workers and has provided quality assurance training for social workers employed in end-stage renal disease programs.[15]

Finally, in the past few years, numerous articles on quality assurance have appeared in the social work literature. Among them are articles describing particular quality assurance systems[16] as well as general issues and trends.[17] Similarly, several

---

[13] Society for Hospital Social Work Directors, *Development of Professional Standards Review for Hospital Social Work* (Chicago: American Hospital Association, 1977).

[14] *See*, for example, William Hall and Gerald St. Dennis, eds., *Accountability: A Critical Issue in Social Services* (Washington, D.C.: Bureau of Community Health Services, U.S. Department of Health, Education & Welfare, 1972); William Hall and Gerald St. Dennis, eds., *Quality Assurance in Social Service Programs for Mothers and Children* (Washington, D.C.: Bureau of Community Health Services, U.S. Department of Health, Education & Welfare, 1975); Robert Jackson and Jean Morton, eds., *Evaluation of Social Work Services in Community Health and Medical Care Programs* (Washington, D.C.: Bureau of Community Health Services, U.S. Department of Health, Education & Welfare, 1973); and Florence Stein, William Hall, and Christine Young, eds., *Working Conference on Minimum Review Criteria for Professional Social Work Practice* (Washington, D.C.: Bureau of Community Health Services, U.S. Department of Health, Education & Welfare, 1976).

[15] California Regional Medical Program, *Project to Develop Model Criteria and Standards for Care of End-Stage Renal Disease Patients* (Oakland, Calif.: Committee on Regional Medical Programs, 1976).

[16] *See*, for example, Roslyn Chernesky and Abraham Lurie, "Developing a Quality Assurance Program," *Health and Social Work*, 1 (February 1976), pp. 117–130; Oystein LaBianca and Gerald Cubelli, "A New Approach to Building Social Work Knowledge," *Social Work in Health Care*, 2 (Winter 1976–1977), pp. 139–152; Kris Ferguson, et al., "Initiation of a Quality Assurance Program for Social Work Practice in a Teaching Hospital," *Social Work in Health Care*, 2 (Winter 1976–1977), pp. 205–217; Barbara Berkman and Helen Rehr, "Social Work Undertakes Its Own Audit," *Social Work in Health Care*, 3 (Spring 1978), pp. 275–286; Robert Spano, Thomas Kiresuk,

sessions at professional meetings have been devoted to this issue, including presentations on quality assurance at the National Conference on Social Welfare and the social work section of the American Public Health Association.

General Trends

Many of the quality assurance activities in other professions are relevant to social work. Many nonphysician health care providers are attempting to define their roles in quality assurance. The federal government, the American Hospital Association, the Joint Commission on Accreditation of Hospitals, and the American Public Health Association all seem to be supporting an interdisciplinary or multidisciplinary approach to quality assurance in hospitals rather than separate review systems.[18]

Among all the health professionals, especially among physicians, controversy continues over whether it is possible to determine what is optimal practice. Some have pointed out that it is not known which poor outcomes actually result from inappropriate process and whether some good outcomes occur even though items of patient management originally considered crucial are missing.[19] These same considerations apply to social work's quality assurance efforts.

---

and Sandor Lund, "An Operational Model to Achieve Accountability for Social Work in Health Care," *Social Work in Health Care,* 3 (Winter 1977), pp. 123–142; Patricia Volland, "Social Work Information and Accountability Systems in a Hospital Setting," *Social Work in Health Care,* 1 (Spring 1976), pp. 277–286; and Jon Keith, "Hospital Social Work Audit Focuses on Discharge Planning," *Hospitals,* 51 (December 1977), pp. 73–75.

[17] *See,* for example, Mildred Reynolds, "Professional Review of Health Care Services," *Health and Social Work,* 1 (November 1976), pp. 38–60; Helen Rehr, "Professional Standards Review: The Challenge to Social Work," and Barbara Berkman, "Are Social Service Audit Systems Feasible? Experiences with a Hospital Based and a Regional Approach," both in *Professional Standards Review for Hospital Social Work,* op. cit., pp. 23–36 and 37–43; Claudia Lorish, "Examining Quality Assurance Systems" *Health and Social Work,* 2 (May 1977), pp. 20–41; and Margaret Wayne, "PSRO: Issues in Health Care Policy," *Health and Social Work,* 2 (November 1977), pp. 25–50.

[18] *See* U.S. Department of Health, Education & Welfare, *Technical Assistance Document No. 9; Hospital Week* (Chicago: American Hospital Association, October 7, 1977); and *The Nation's Health* (September 1977), p. 5.

[19] "Letters," *Journal of the American Medical Association,* 238 (August 8, 1977), pp. 470–480.

Terminology

Quality assurance has necessitated the development of some new concepts and terminology and the adaptation of some existing ones. Some of the terms and concepts have their origins in the PSRO legislation; others predate PSRO and come from the management, planning, and research areas. For purposes of this study, it is necessary to define some of these terms. It is recognized that these terms are used by professionals in a variety of ways and that not everyone will agree with the definitions presented here. However, these definitions are based on a review of PSRO regulations; JCAH materials; social work, medical, and research literature; and definitions provided by survey respondents. It should be noted that there was substantial disagreement among survey respondents about the meaning of some of these terms.

Quality assurance refers to activities designed to assess services systematically, to determine whether they comply with what are believed to be adequate services, and to correct any observed deficiencies. *Evaluation* designates the general process of judging the worthwhileness of an activity.[20] *Evaluative research* refers to the use of the scientific method for the specific purpose of making an evaluation.[21] Evaluation is identical to the assessment portion of quality assurance. Quality assurance, in other words, consists of evaluation and corrective action.

Peer review refers to a set of procedures by which a group of professional peers evaluate the quality of care delivered to patients and determine whether corrective action is needed. It usually consists of identifying the operational indicators of adequate care, reviewing care to see whether these indicators are present, and recommending solutions whenever care is less than adequate. The actual review of care can be done either concurrently or retrospectively and can review the work of an individual or a whole department. *Concurrent review* refers to the assessment of care conducted while the patient is still receiving care. Such an assessment may contain *utilization reviews*, which examine the services patients are receiving and

---

[20] Edward Suchman, *Evaluative Research* (New York: Russell Sage Foundation, 1967), p. 7.

[21] Ibid.

judge whether these services are necessary, as well as reviews of other aspects of care. *Retrospective review* refers to an evaluation of care conducted on a sample of patients after their receipt of service; it is usually an in-depth study. Such a retrospective study is often called a *medical care evaluation study* in PSRO terminology and a *medical audit* in JCAH terminology.

Most peer review systems contain criteria to be used in evaluating care. *Criteria* are predetermined indicators against which aspects of actual care can be compared to judge their quality. They may be derived from *norms* that are numerical or statistical measures of usual, observed performance. For each criterion, a *standard* may be specified. A standard is the range of acceptable variation from the criterion.

Reviews may be conducted independently by each profession or jointly by several professions. An *interdisciplinary* review consists of a single set of criteria that are applicable to the combined work of an entire team of professionals from several disciplines. *Multidisciplinary* reviews refer to several separate sets of criteria, each from a different profession, that are applied simultaneously to a group of cases.

Patient information systems, as they relate to quality assurance, are ongoing mechanisms for systematically gathering, analyzing, and reporting data on the care of patients. They should be distinguished from organizational information systems that collect data on the administration of programs.[22] The data may include patients' characteristics, patients' problems, the services received, and the results of service. These systems may contribute to quality assurance in several ways. First, practice patterns can be quantified to produce norms. Second, profiles of patients' problems, services received, and results of services can be examined to identify areas needing in-depth study. Such an examination is referred to as *profile analysis* in PSRO terminology. Third, the data can be analyzed to determine the effectiveness of services in producing desired outcomes. Such an analysis can serve as the assessment component of quality assurance and lead to corrective action. If it is so used, it is a medical care evaluation study, although the

---

[22] Gary and Margaret Bowers, *Cultivating Client Information Systems* (Washington, D.C.: Department of Health, Education & Welfare, 1977).

11

method differs from the more prevalent peer review approach.

Quality assurance programs may have one or more focuses. Components that focus on *structure* examine program inputs, such as training, personnel, materials, resources, time, administrative practices, and the like, to see whether they are adequate.[23] Other components focus on *process,* that is, on actual service activities.[24] They look to see whether what is believed to be good practice has actually been applied. Another possible focus is *outcome,* which is the impact of the service on the client.[25] Components with this focus look to see whether the results achieved may be termed acceptable. Some components focus on *access* to services to see whether the population believed to require services has actually had the opportunity to receive them. Finally, quality assurance may focus on the *linkage* between intervention and outcome to determine what service activities, under what circumstances, are likely to produce certain outcomes.[26]

---

[23] Avedes Donabedian, "Evaluating the Quality of Medical Care," *Millbank Memorial Fund Quarterly,* 44 (Spring 1966), p. 170.

[24] Ibid., p. 169.

[25] Ibid., p. 168.

[26] Lorish, op. cit.

3
METHODOLOGY

THE MAIN PURPOSES of this study were to describe and compare some existing quality assurance programs in social work and to identify similarities and differences among them. It was expected that such an analysis would be useful to social workers beginning to develop quality assurance programs in their facilities and that it would lead to some uniform standards for quality assurance programs in social work. It was not the intention to produce or recommend an entire model program or to make an exhaustive survey of the incidence or prevalence of quality assurance activities in social work.

Design and Sampling

Since the purposes of this study were to explore and describe, a comparative case study approach was used. Case examples to be included in the study were identified in several ways:
- The files at NASW were reviewed to identify groups that reported implementing quality assurance programs.
- The Society for Hospital Social Work Directors identified groups that had implemented programs.
- The social work literature was reviewed to locate reports of quality assurance programs.
- The author attended the annual meetings of the Society for Hospital Social Work Directors and the American Public Health Association and located additional programs through informal contacts. The cases selected were limited to those programs that had been tested and at least partially implemented.

These procedures resulted in the identification of twenty-seven programs. The regional distribution of those programs is presented in Table 1. Although attempts were made to locate more programs outside the Northeast and Midwest, few were identified as a result of these extra efforts. It is not clear whether quality assurance programs are actually less prevalent in the South and West or whether such programs are less likely to become known to the professional organizations based in the Northeast and Midwest.

TABLE 1. REGIONAL DISTRIBUTION OF PROGRAMS STUDIED

Region	Number
Northeast	12
Midwest	7
South	5
West	3
Total	27

Obviously, then, this sample was not selected to be representative of quality assurance programs throughout the country. Rather, it was selected to conduct a more in-depth examination of a few programs that had been tested and implemented and to identify similarities and differences. Therefore, from the findings presented here, no generalizations will be drawn about the number or distribution of social work quality assurance programs around the country.

Data Collection and Analysis

To gather comparable information on the quality assurance programs, an interview schedule was developed and pretested on a group of hospital social work directors (see Appendix A). This interview schedule was designed to elicit the following information:

●The nature of the setting in which the program was developed, tested, and implemented.

●The purposes for which it was developed and the major assumptions on which it was based.

14

●The activities that went into the development of the program.

●The components of the program and their content and operation.

●The costs of developing and operating the program.

●The usefulness of the program.

One or more informants were interviewed for each program identified. The persons interviewed were those who had major responsibility for program development or, in some cases, had been designated by a development group as spokesperson. It was common, however, for many people to have participated in the development of each program. Appendix B lists the programs studied and their spokesperson. In addition to the interviews, forms used in the program and other descriptive materials were obtained from some informants.

The descriptive materials and the results of the interviews were analyzed both quantitatively and qualitatively. The goal was not to describe a specific program, but to identify similarities and differences among programs and to derive some general trends and principles from these findings. The findings are reported in Chapter 4.

4
ANALYSIS OF PROGRAMS

THE TWENTY-SEVEN quality assurance programs were compared to answer several questions.

- How were these programs developed?
- What are their basic assumptions?
- What are their major components?
- What are the characteristics of each component?
- What are the advantages and disadvantages of different approaches?
- What are the factors that affect costs?
- What are the effects of these programs?

The results of these comparisons and the questions and issues they raise are presented in this chapter.

Characteristics of Settings

The programs examined were developed and tested in a variety of settings. Many were developed and tested in general teaching hospitals, government hospitals, and community hospitals, but one program had been developed exclusively for an ambulatory facility. Many of the hospitals involved had more than 750 beds, although one program was developed exclusively for small hospitals (Program 16) and several others were developed in smaller hospitals. The size of the social work departments involved ranged from 5 to 198 workers with a substantial minority having fewer than 20 workers. The program with 198 workers was implemented in three administratively related facilities.

Program Development

Although a few quality assurance programs emerged as early as 1967, the majority were started around 1974. Three-quarters of the programs studied were developed in individual hospitals rather than as regionwide programs. About 80 percent were developed by social work staff, and a few were assisted by medical records, nursing, or administrative staff or outside consultants. The consensus of social workers served as the most common basis for developing criteria, although, for a few programs, some criteria were based on data that was collected on actual social work activities.

General Assumptions

An important question for quality assurance programs is whether one can judge the quality of service by looking at what the worker did or whether it is necessary to look at what happened to the client as a result of the service. In other words, should quality be judged by looking at the social work process or the client outcome? About 70 percent of the respondents reported that their programs were based on the assumption that quality could be judged by comparing what the workers did with some standard of what ought to have been done, that is, a focus on process. The other 30 percent assumed that because of uncertainty about what interventions produce desired results, programs must examine client outcomes to see whether desired results are actually achieved (focus on outcome). In reality many quality assurance programs used aspects of both focuses.

Components of Programs

The quality assurance programs reviewed each contained one or more components. These components can be divided into three categories:

Information system. An ongoing mechanism for collecting, storing, and analyzing patient-related information.

Peer review system. A set of procedures by which a group of professional peers evaluate the quality of care delivered to patients.

Guaranteed access system. A mechanism for assuring that patients who need social work services actually receive them.

Table 2 summarizes the components contained in each program studied. A detailed discussion of each component follows, including examples drawn from the programs examined. A description of the operation of a fictitious program appears in Appendix C.

INFORMATION SYSTEMS

The information systems described here are patient related. Although these systems can produce information related exclusively to the provider, they take the individual case as their primary unit of analysis. Certain other statistical reporting systems store information according to provider. Eleven of the programs reviewed contained an information system component. The data contained in such systems usually included (1) the physical and demographic characteristics of patients, (2) patients' problems or the goals of service, (3) the types and frequency of activities or services of workers, and (4) the outcome for the patient (for example, resolution of the problem or attainment of the goal). The information system's data base was maintained and updated through special forms completed by workers. These forms could be patient specific or worker specific. In either case, there was a mechanism for bringing together all the information on each patient and storing it in that way.

Use of the system. The patient-related information system has the potential to answer questions about the quality of social work being delivered. In the programs reviewed, the systems were used to describe the following:

●Patterns of social workers' activities, by client characteristics and problems or by worker.

●The frequency or time devoted to various services or problems by each worker.

●The general outlines of client outcomes, that is, the extent to which goals were achieved or problems resolved, by worker, by service, or by problem category.

These kinds of analyses were found useful for a variety of purposes, such as:

18

•To identify types of patients, problems, or services in which outcomes were unacceptable. These categories were then studied in further detail in peer review.

•To identify norms of practice, such as the average amount of time that was devoted to a particular service or the types of services usually directed toward certain problems. These findings were used to guide peer review.

•To identify workers whose outcomes were unacceptable or whose utilization of time was widely different from others. These workers were then studied further or given assistance.

One potentially important question for social work practice does not seem to have been asked of these data bases: What kinds of interventions lead to what outcomes for what kinds of patients? Such a question requires multivariate analysis and could contribute to the development of practice theory in health care. These findings could also guide the setting of process criteria to be used in peer review. Establishing process criteria in this way would strengthen their validity since the criteria would be based on evidence that they lead to desired outcomes.

Data processing. Of the eleven programs that had information-system components, five processed data manually, and six used electronic data processing. Each computer system analyzed the data with programs developed specifically for that information system, although some systems used modifications of programs developed for other information systems. The cost of writing these programs ranged from tens of thousands of dollars to less than one thousand dollars. The modification of an existing program was likely to produce substantially lower costs than the creation of a new one.

The departments that operated their information systems manually were severely limited in the types of relationships they could examine and the types of questions they could answer. Since many manual systems used a single form for each patient and obtained all necessary data elements on that form, the data in most such systems could probably be fed into a computer and analyzed using a standard statistical program package.[1] Since there would be no cost for developing a computer program, the only cost would be for key punching and

---

[1] See, for example, Norman Nie et al., *Statistical Package for the Social Sciences* (New York: McGraw-Hill Book Co., 1975).

TABLE 2. COMPONENTS OF QUALITY ASSURANCE PROGRAMS

Program Number	Group	Information System	Peer Review	Access	Criteria	Focus of Criteria	Format	Computerized	Number of Beds	Type of Hospital
1	Memphis City Hospital	No	Yes	No	Specific	Process/outcome	JCAH	No	1,000+	Teaching/governmental
2	Stamford Hospital	No	Yes	No	General and specific	Process/outcome	JCAH	No	250–500	Teaching
3	New England region	Yes	No	No	Not applicable	Not applicable	Not applicable	Yes	Range	All adult
4	Massachusetts General Hospital	Yes	Yes	No	General and specific	Process	Unique	Yes	1,000+	Teaching
5	Mt. Sinai Hospital	Yes	Yes	Yes	General	Process	Unique	Yes	1,000+	Teaching
6	University of Virginia Medical Center	Yes	Yes	Yes	General	Process	JCAH	No	501–750	Teaching
7	University of Michigan Medical Center	No	Yes	No	Specific	Process	Unique	No	751–1,000	Teaching
8	Connecticut Region	Yes	No	No	Not applicable	Not applicable	Not applicable	No	Range	All adult
9	Strong Memorial Hospital	Yes	Yes	No	Specific	Process/outcome	JCAH	Yes	751–1,000	Teaching
10	Cincinnati General Hospital	No	Yes	Yes	General and specific	Process	JCAH and unique	No	501–750	Teaching
11	Children's Medical Center, Dallas	Yes	Yes	Yes	General	Process	Unique	No	101–250	Pediatric
12	E. W. Sparrow Hospital	Yes	Yes	Yes	General and specific	Process/outcome	JCAH	No	251–500	Teaching
13	Johns Hopkins Hospital	Yes	Yes	Yes	Specific	Process	Unique	Yes	1,000+	Teaching

TABLE 2. (Continued)

Program Number	Group	Information System	Peer Review	Access	Criteria	Focus of Criteria	Format	Computerized	Number of Beds	Type of Hospital
14	Hospital of University of Pennsylvania	No	Yes	Yes	General	Process	Unique	No	501–750	Teaching
15	Beth Israel Hospital	No	Yes	Yes	General	Process	Unique	No	251–500	Teaching
16	Philadelphia's Small Hospitals	No	Yes	No	General	Process	Unique	No	101–500	Community
17	University of Minnesota Hospital	Yes	Yes	No	Specific	Process	JCAH	Yes	501–750	Teaching
18	Long Island Jewish Hospital	No	Yes	No	General	Process/outcome	Unique	No	1,000+	Teaching
19	Cuyahoga County Hospital	No	Yes	No	General	Process	Unique	No	751–1,000	Teaching/governmental
20	Cook City Hospital	No	Yes	Yes	Specific	Process	JCAH	No	1,000+	Governmental
21	University of Maryland Hospital	Yes	Yes	Yes	General and specific	Process	Unique	No	501–750	Teaching/governmental
22	Cleveland Maternal and Infant Project	No	Yes	No	General	Process/outcome	Unique	No	Ambulatory	Governmental
23	Denver Department of Hospitals	Yes	Yes	Yes	General and specific	Process	JCAH	No	251–500	Teaching/governmental
24	Harborview Medical Center	Yes	No	No	Not applicable	Not applicable	Not applicable	No	251–500	Teaching
25	Martin Luther King Hospital	Yes	Yes	Yes	General and specific	Process	Unique	Yes	251–500	Teaching
26	Richland Memorial Hospital	No	Yes	No	General and specific	Process	JCAH and unique	No	501–750	Teaching
27	Hillcrest Hospital	No	Yes	No	General	Process	Unique	No	501–750	Teaching

computer time. If the computer used is relatively efficient, the processing costs in a department with about five hundred case closures a month could be less than one hundred dollars a month. This processing cost would, no doubt, be offset by the decreased clerical time and the increased analytic capacity. Most universities have a number of these statistical packages available, and their simpler uses can be learned by anyone with a beginning knowledge of research and statistics.

A difficult problem in developing a social work information system is to obtain a useful, valid, and reliable measurement of the important variables or data elements.[2] Even recording simple physical and demographic characteristics of patients, such as age, sex, race, income, marital status, and medical diagnosis, requires training people in the exact meaning of the coding system.

Client problems. Classifying client problems has proved to be a most difficult task. The categories developed must not only be mutually exclusive and exhaustive, but also meaningful to social work practice. There must be some principle of classification that prevents the mixing of apples and oranges. Categories may be deduced from theories of human behavior or the experience of practitioners. Alternatively, they may be created by induction, that is, by classifying patients' concrete statements of problems.

Most of the information systems examined had a problem taxonomy. Some examples of lists of problems appear in Table 3, and several have been shortened to facilitate presentation here. Most were derived from the experience of workers, but at least two were based on a theory of casework (Programs 9 and 25). There were some similarities among these problem taxonomies. In all systems some categories reflected deficiencies in the capacity or functioning of the patient, some reflected deficiencies in the resources of the environment or excessive environmental demands, and others reflected discrepancies or incongruencies between the patient and the environment. The problems listed could also be grouped according to the aspect of functioning that was affected—physical, economic, emotional, social, or behavioral.

[2] Barbara Berkman and Helen Rehr, "Seven Steps to Audit," *Social Work in Health Care,* 2 (Spring 1978), pp. 295–305.

A common difficulty in some of these problem lists was the tendency to mix patients' problems with social work activities. Problem lists should ideally reflect characteristics of patients, that is, the problems they are experiencing. It was often difficult to separate these characteristics from the social work service that would be delivered to reduce the problems. However, this is an important conceptual distinction. If social workers define patients' problems only in terms of the services they offer, they will never learn about the existence of problems for which they have no service. Further, a given problem might commonly be addressed by several types of service. One of the services might be more effective in solving the problem than another, but if problems are defined only as the need for a particular service, such a finding could never emerge.

Another difficulty in constructing lists of problems is determining the number of categories to include. Too many categories may make meaningful analysis difficult because the number of people experiencing certain problems is too small. Further, when the number of categories is larger, workers will be less reliable in their judgments of which category to assign a particular patient.[3] On the other hand, too few categories will end up mixing together problems that have different implications for social work practice.

One solution to establishing categories may be to have initially a long and detailed list of concrete problems. Each patient would be assigned a "1" if he or she had the problem and a "0" if he or she did not. After data are collected on a large and representative group of patients, a factor analysis or other similar technique might be used to discover which of these concrete problems cluster together in the real world. The clusters could then become the problem categories to be used in the future.

No matter which list of problems is used, it is necessary that each category be defined precisely. If social workers do not share the same definitions, there is no assurance that they are placing the same problems in the same categories. About three-quarters of the lists of problems had detailed definitions (see Appendix D for an example of a detailed problem list).

---

[3] At least one system (Program 5) has studied the reliability of its problem taxonomy and found it acceptable.

TABLE 3. EXAMPLES OF PROBLEM TAXONOMIES

Program 23	Programs 3 and 5	Program 11
Health care	Complaints related to hospital service from patient or family	Understand: Medical/physical condition; Treatment plan
Overutilization	Concrete aids medically recommended (e.g., appliances, telephones, prosthesis)	Carry out medical plan: Administer medicine; Utilize equipment; Follow orders specific to diagnosis
Underutilization	Coordinated Home Care (formal program) needed	Financial ability to get: Diet; Medicine; Transportation; Clothing; Shelter
Nursing home	Family interrelationships adversely affect patient's condition and/or response to treatment	Community resources: Availability; Can family use?
Boarding care	Financial problems (may or may not be result of illness)	Emotional response: Caretaker's attitude toward patient; Acceptance of disability; Support of child
Homemaker/home care	Health education including psychosocial supports	
Medical equipment	High social risk that precipitates need for health care (e.g., drug abuse, alcoholism)	
Physical rehabilitation	Home supports needed (e.g., homemaker, home health aid, baby-sitter, day care, recreation)	
Vocational rehabilitation	Housing unsuitable for continuing needs (e.g., too many stairs, inadequate kitchen)	
Aging	Legal services needed	
Adult neglect	Long-term institutional care (e.g., extended care facility, skilled nursing home, intermediate care facility, rest home, chronic hospital)	
Adult assault	Patient/family depressed, angry, fearful, anxious about diagnostic/medical procedures and so forth	
Abortion		
Child abuse		
Nonaccidental trauma		
Child neglect		
Failure to thrive		
Mental retardation		
Developmental deviation		
Familial/marital		

TABLE 3. (*Continued*)

Program 23	Programs 3 and 5	Program 11
Parent/child relationship	Patient/family depressed, fearful, anxious about prognosis, dying, and so forth	Supportive relationships to patient: Extended family Social School Work
Parental (e.g., unmarried parenthood)	Patient/family having psychosocial problems as a result of illness (family must assume new roles)	
Child care		Family relationships: Stability of marital relationship
Relinquishment	Patient/family problems not related to illness	Sources of emotional support for parental figures
School	Patient/family reactions cause problems for staff, e.g., acting-out behavior, discharge against medical advice	Sharing responsibilities in the family
Behavioral problems		Ability of each parenting figure to individualize
Emotional disturbance	Rehabilitative services needed (occupational therapy and physical therapy)	
Psychosomatic		
Adjustment reaction	Sheltered care needed (e.g., foster home, halfway house)	
Interpersonal relationships	Temporary institutional care away from home (e.g., convalescent care, other hospitals)	
Alcoholism and drug abuse		
Suicidal	Transportation services needed	
Legal	Visiting nurse services needed	
Immigration problems		
Financial/food	Vocational services needed (may or may not be result of illness or disability)	
Housing		
Employment/unemployment	Other (specify, e.g., evaluation only)	
Transportation		
Recreation/social isolation		
Non-English speaking		
Outreach		

25

TABLE 3. (Continued)

Program 13[a]	Program 12[a]	Program 17
Family relationships	Impaired behavior	Adjustment to health problems
Living conditions	Impaired health behavior	Anxiety reactions
Individual/family functioning related to illness	Educational deficits	Behavioral problems
Difficulties in interpersonal relationships	Family impairment/deficits	Chemical use
Temporary financial crisis	Cultural conflicts	Education
Medical insurance coverage	Religious deficits/conflicts	Environmental problems
Lack of knowledge of community resources	Living conditions/deficits	Family/marital
Other special conditions	Lack of financial resources	Financial
Behavior symptomatology	Employment difficulties	Placement
Thought/mood disturbance	Legal complications	Psychotic symptoms
	Deficits in community resources	Self-concept
	Deficits in transportation	Sexuality
		Child Abuse
		Continuity of care
		Decision making
		Depression
		Health maintenance
		Interpersonal relationships and social activities
		Legal
		Physical complaints and characteristics
		Social service evaluation
		Suicide
		Treatment complications

Programs 9 and 25[b]	Program 24
Interpersonal conflict	Special interactional dysfunction (in hospital)
Dissatisfaction in social relations	Social interactional dysfunction (outside)
Problems with formal organizations	Affective behavior
Difficulties in role performance	Activities, work, school
Problems of social transition	Financial
Reactive emotional distress	Living arrangements
Inadequate resources	Physical needs
Intrapersonal conflict	
Other	

[a] Only major categories are presented here, but these systems had several subcategories within each category.
[b] This system was adapted from that described by William Reid and Laura Epstein in *Task Centered Casework* (New York: Columbia University Press, 1972).

26

Services received. Another element contained in most information systems was some indication of the nature of the worker's activities with or on behalf of the patient. These activities were classified along several dimensions, including the following: the type of service given, the frequency or number of service units delivered, the duration of service, and the target of service—the patient, the patient's family, the community, other hospital personnel, and so on. Units of service were frequently computed in fifteen-minute intervals making time measurement fairly straightforward.[4] Specifying the targets of service was usually quite direct and simple also. The major difficulty arose in specifying the type of service, and some modified examples of service taxonomies are presented in Table 4.

The difficulty arises because social workers usually engage in a variety of activities on behalf of patients, and these activities are often clustered together to form a package that may be labeled a service.[5] For example, discharge planning is a common service category. To deliver this service the worker may engage in multiple activities, including (1) case-finding, (2) assessment, (3) exploration of the family's feelings, perceptions, and capacity to provide needed support, (4) arrangement of community resources, and (5) counseling the patient and/or family to increase the capacity to cope with discharge. Some service classification systems may place these activities in separate categories, others do not. For example, some systems see assessment and counseling as an unspecified component of all social work services (Program 12, for example); others (Program 23, for example) report these as separate activities. Further, some systems partially combine the type of service with the problem toward which the service is directed (Program 6).

As with problem taxonomies, the key to making service classification systems reliable is to have a precise definition of each service to differentiate it from all other services. Many of the systems reviewed provided such definitions and trained all workers in applying them. Program 25 provided a list of

---

[4] Such approaches are consistent with those described in Society for Hospital Social Work Directors, *A Reporting System for Hospital Social Workers* (Chicago: American Hospital Association, 1978), p. 16.

[5] The classifications discussed here are only those for case services; they exclude workers' activities not directed toward or on behalf of particular patients.

27

TABLE 4. EXAMPLES OF SERVICE TAXONOMIES

Program 9	Program 17	Program 13	Program 23
Discharge planning/coordination	Information/screening/referral	Patient movement—admission	Consultation
Continued care planning/ coordination (outpatient)	Problem assessment/evaluation	Patient movement—discharge	Health maintenance
Psychosocial evaluation only	Counseling	Other health planning	Case conference
Psychosocial treatment (patient)	Rehabilitation/restoration/habilitation	Evaluation/information	Outreach
Psychosocial treatment (family)	Care services	Counseling—illness	Referral
Psychosocial treatment (group)	Patient-client–related case preparation and	Counseling—psychosocial	Support
Case consultation	record keeping	Counseling—situational	Facilitative
Advocacy		Provision material help	Coordination
Other		Referral to community	Assessment
		Coordination services	Translation
		Other	Family therapy
			Individual therapy
			Group therapy
			Other

Program 3	Program 12	Program 6
Advocacy services	Assess individual and family functioning	Social evaluation and assessment
Discharge planning	Assess continuity of care needs	Help with psychosocial functioning
Follow-up (if planned)	Implement social components of home care	Help with adaptation to illness
Home visit	Assist with transfer to nursing facility	Help with posthospital planning
Intrahospital referral	Assist with transfer to another hospital	Facilitating services
Psychosocial evaluation	Assist with transfer to adult foster care	
Treatment-family sessions	Assist with utilization problems	Program 24
Treatment-group work for patient and/or family	Facilitate use of financial resources	Assessment
Intradepartmental collaboration	Assist with care of family members	Intervention
Interagency or interfacility conferences	Respond to legal needs	Consultation
Referral to other agency or facility	Provide illness-related education and information	
Interdisciplinary conferences	Assist with planning after death	Program 25
Social service consultations	Refer to other community resources	Intake services
	Participate in rehabilitation process	Information and referral services
	Provide therapy	Treatment services
	Arrange transportation	Supportive services
		Community services

28

numerous and detailed actions that fell within each category. A comparison of the sets of definitions used in different programs suggested that many terms had meanings that varied from program to program. Common usage, therefore, cannot be assumed across settings.

Client outcome.   Another variable frequently measured in social work information systems is client outcome. Most of the programs reviewed measured outcome by looking at the resolution of problems. Frequently, when the case was closed, the worker was asked to judge the extent to which each problem had been resolved. A four-point scale of problem resolution was most common. Program 13, for example, rated each problem (1) resolved, (2) decreasing, (3) no change, or (4) increasing.

Program 11 took a slightly different approach. At the time each case was opened, the worker was asked to rate the patient's functioning in each problem area as (1) unsatisfactory, (2) marginal, (3) satisfactory, or (4) excellent. At closing, the same problems were rated again. The difference between pretreatment and posttreatment problem status was taken as an indicator of outcome. Program 17 used goal attainment scaling as an indicator of client outcome. This is a technique in which treatment goals are set by workers and patients at the beginning of treatment. At this time, possible outcomes for each goal are stated in terms of concrete, observable behaviors. These outcomes are distributed along a scale from the most unfavorable outcome thought likely to the most favorable outcome thought likely. At the end of the treatment, the degree of goal attainment is assessed and a score derived.

The measurement of client outcomes is an important element in quality assurance, since the purpose of social work is to produce desirable results for patients. High-quality social work services, then, are those that lead to desirable outcomes. However, many factors influence the outcome of social work services aside from the activities of the social worker. Especially important are the environmental resources available to the patient and his or her own capacities. Thus, although it is desirable to examine social work outcomes and their relationship to social work activities, the precise effect of social work services can only be assessed in studies that control for client capacity and community resources. Only in such studies can several types of intervention be compared.

The review of the eleven information systems in the programs studied suggested that such systems have the capacity to yield a wealth of information about the effectiveness and efficiency of social work services. They can identify areas that may be receiving poor service or lack resources and that need further investigation. They can identify services that hold promise of being effective for certain kinds of problems. However, the ex post facto nature of the information systems usually prevents them from yielding conclusive evidence of causal relationships between social work services and client outcomes.

PEER REVIEW

A second component of quality assurance programs was peer review. This refers to an examination of the quality of care provided for patients that is conducted by a professional's own peers. Almost all twenty-five programs reviewed had this component. These peer review systems were compared along a number of dimensions.

Development of criteria.   To examine the quality of care, the peer group must develop criteria that can be applied to actual care. One way to develop criteria for quality assurance systems is to obtain a consensus of professionals. Such criteria reflect the predominant beliefs of the profession about what constitutes acceptable practice. When the knowledge of the profession is accurate and complete, such an approach is likely to produce valid criteria, that is, criteria that distinguish adequate from inadequate practice. If there is a high degree of agreement in the profession concerning facts and values, the criteria that emerge are likely to be fairly precise. However, if there is a lack of agreement in the profession, criteria may be ambiguous. When the knowledge guiding the criteria is inaccurate or incomplete, the criteria may be invalid.

Consider, for example, the problem of setting criteria for the content of a social history. If social workers from both behavioral and psychoanalytic perspectives are asked to develop such criteria, they may disagree somewhat. Criteria acceptable to both groups may be ambiguous. In addition, if the two perspectives result in different criteria, it is difficult to determine which are valid in the sense of identifying those social histories that have a higher probability of producing desired results.

A second approach to developing criteria is empirical. In this case, criteria are derived from actual practice and may be based on statistical averages. For example, if the average time between the initial referral and the time a social worker sees a family is twenty-four hours, this could be used as a criterion for judging practice. Cases that exceed this time by a given amount can be judged unacceptable. Although the average practice is not necessarily acceptable, this criterion can be further validated empirically by seeing whether cases complying with this criterion are more likely to achieve certain results (a timely discharge, for example) than cases that do not.

Almost all the systems reviewed used a consensus approach to the development of criteria. However, several programs with information systems reported they would eventually provide empirical findings to guide the development of criteria for the peer review system.

Focus of criteria. A second basis for comparing peer review systems is the focus of the criteria. Criteria for peer review can focus on process or outcome. Process criteria involve looking at actual social work practice to determine to what degree certain elements or activities necessary for good quality care have actually occurred. Some systems judged only whether the action had occurred; others asked for a judgment about whether something had been done "correctly" or "adequately" or "appropriately." This judgment might be qualitative or quantitative. Most peer review criteria examined were of the process variety.

Outcome criteria look at whether desired results have occurred. The outcomes examined may be immediate or ultimate, but they are usually short-term outcomes in hospital social work. To illustrate a distinction between process and outcome criteria, the following examples are offered:

●Process criterion: The worker explores the patient's feelings about home care.

●Outcome criterion: The patient verbalizes acceptance of the home care plan.

Only a few sets of true outcome criteria for peer review were discovered.

Application of criteria. A third distinction among peer review systems is whether the criteria are applied by social workers or by other hospital personnel. Only four systems used medical records analysts to apply the criteria, and the rest mainly used social workers to conduct reviews. When medical records analysts conducted the initial reviews, the cases not meeting the criteria were referred to a professional team for analysis.

A fourth dimension of peer review is whether the criteria are applied to the medical record or to some other instrument. All systems examined reviewed the medical record. In those institutions that maintained dual records, some peer review systems also reviewed social work records. Two programs (5 and 1) included a patient satisfaction instrument, administered after discharge, as an indicator of quality.

A fifth dimension of peer review systems is the format used for the application of criteria to the medical record. Seven departments had done at least one review using the JCAH format for medical audits. The others used a variety of approaches, many bearing a resemblance to the JCAH format. The JCAH format specifies each criterion, the exceptions to that criterion, and the instructions to the reviewer for determining whether the criterion was met. An example of this format appears in Table 5. Since retrieval instructions are specific in this format, this approach is most useful when the criteria are to be applied by medical records analysts or other non-social work personnel and will, in general, be highly reliable.

TABLE 5. EXAMPLES OF CRITERIA IN JCAH FORMAT

Element	Exceptions	Instructions
Interview patient within three working days of referral[a]	Patient refuses interview Patient discharged Patient deceased Patient transferred	Look for a progress note documenting that worker had verbal contact with patient within three days
Document outcomes of identified problems[b]	Death of patient within forty-eight hours Patient left against medical advice Patient declined social services	Look for a statement of resolution of each problem or a statement of improvement or outcome

[a] Criterion taken from Program 17.
[b] Criterion taken from Program 12.

A sixth distinction among peer review programs is whether the criteria are general or specific. General criteria are applicable to all types of patients; specific criteria are applicable only to certain groups of patients. Fifteen systems had devel-

TABLE 6. (*Continued*)

Program Number	Initial Contact	Assessment/Diagnosis	Treatment Plan/Goals	Service Delivery	Termination/Outcome
16	Is date of initial contact noted? Is reason for initial contact clear? Are there indicators of the need for earlier social service entry? If yes, who caused delay? Patient? Physician? Social Worker? Is the service clear?	Is there some assessment? Does the assessment reflect some understanding of the patient's situation and problem? Is the assessment adequate in terms of the problems the worker identified? Does the assessment include social and physical functioning of the patient? Does the assessment show an understanding of the illness or disability and its implications? Does the worker give his impressions regarding the patient's family? Is it clear which problems will be the focus of the social work intervention? Were the appropriate problems selected for intervention?	Is there an adequate treatment plan? Does the plan reflect patient interest and priority in contrast to hospital interest or priority?	Are social work interventions identified? Are the social work interventions consistent with the plan? Does the intervention indicate adequate involvement with the health care team? Does the intervention indicate adequate involvement with appropriate family members? Does the intervention indicate adequate involvement of appropriate agencies? Where relevant, does the intervention take into account new developments in patient's situation? Are any changes in plan or goal adequately explained? Did this case receive sufficient social work attention?	Was there an appropriate disposition of the case? Is there a closing note? Does the closing note summarize the handling of problems, outcome, reasons for closing, and future planning where relevant?

TABLE 6. (Continued)

Program Number	Initial Contact	Assessment/Diagnosis	Treatment Plan/Goals	Service Delivery	Termination/Outcome
12	Is there documentation of referral assessment? Is there acknowledgment of documentation within two working days?	Is there a statement of problem related to hospitalization and care of patient? Is there subjective or objective data which verifies or validates problem statement?	Is there a statement of goals or plans or of proposed actions by the patient or the social worker on behalf of the patient?	Is there a record of action taken or services provided by the social worker?	Is there documentation of the outcomes for the identified problems?
5[a]	Is the date of initial contact with social work service noted? Is the reason for initial contact clear? Is the source clear (how social service became involved)? Is the opening statement adequate? Did social service enter at the appropriate time and/or point? If no, is it clear why social service entry was not earlier?	Is there evidence of an initial assessment? Is there evidence of an ongoing assessment? Is the assessment adequate in terms of the problem identified by the worker? Does the assessment reflect adequate understanding of the patient's situation/problem? Does the assessment include (a) psychological, (b) social, and (c) physical functioning of patient? Does the assessment show an understanding of the medical condition and its implications?	Is there indication that a contract (mutual agreement on goals between worker and patient/family) has been established? If so, is there justification for patient or family not participating in contract? Was the contract established with the appropriate individual? Is there evidence of adequate patient/family involvement to establish the contract? Is the contract appropriate? Is the contract adequate? Does the contract reflect patient interest/priority rather than agency interest/priority?	Are social work interventions identified? Are interventions noted in a way that is helpful to others? Are social work interventions consistent with the contract? Are social work interventions consistent with the treatment plan? Does the intervention indicate adequate involvement of appropriate family members? Does intervention indicate adequate involvement of appropriate professionals? Where relevant, does intervention take into account new developments in situation?	Was there an appropriate disposition of the case?

TABLE 6. (*Continued*)

Program Number	Initial Contact	Assessment/Diagnosis	Treatment Plan/Goals	Service Delivery	Termination/Outcome
		Does the worker give his/her impression of the patient/family? Is it clear which problems will be the focus of social work intervention? Were the appropriate problems selected for intervention? Have all appropriate problems been selected for intervention?	Should there have been a treatment plan? If yes, is there an adequate treatment plan? Where relevant, are discrepancies between the contract and treatment plan explained?	Are any changes in plan, goals, or contract adequately explained? Is there evidence of a good working relationship between worker and patient/family? Did this case receive sufficient social work attention? Is there evidence of communication between social worker and physician? Was the timing of the collaboration appropriate? Is there evidence of adequate ongoing collaboration with physician? Was there adequate collaboration with other disciplines? Is there evidence of an effective interdisciplinary working relationship?	

[a] This list was modified for presentation here.

37

TABLE 6. (*Continued*)

Program Number	Initial Contact	Assessment/Diagnosis	Treatment Plan/Goals	Service Delivery	Termination/Outcome
15	Does initial note state reason for referral and by whom?	Does subjective information include: a. A clear description of patient's perception of the problem? b. An appropriate past history and assessment of the current situation? Does objective information document observable affect, defenses, and mental status? a. Is the worker's assessment a logical outcome of the subjective and objective data? b. Does the worker's formulation of the problem indicate diagnostic thinking?	Are goals clearly stated? Implied? Neither? Are they an appropriate and logical outcome of the worker's assessment? Are the goals a direct response to the reason for referral? If not, is there an explanation for change of focus? Are there recommendations for management techniques that could be useful to other providers?	Is subsequent social work activity noted within the required period? Does the activity follow the stated goals? If not, does the subsequent note indicate reasons for the goal changes?	Is there a closing note? Does it indicate successful intervention? If there are remaining problems, are these noted and the reason for closing the case explained?

38

TABLE 6. (*Continued*)

Program Number	Initial Contact	Assessment/Diagnosis	Treatment Plan/Goals	Service Delivery	Termination/Outcome
21	Was this an appropriate case for the department? Does case meet content and objective criteria?	Does subjective information include: a. A clear description of patient's perception of the problem, and if not, is there a clinical explanation? b. Appropriate past history and current situation? Does objective information document significant observable behaviors (affect, defense, mental status) or is there an explanation of why this is not included? Does formulation of problems or conclusion indicate accurate diagnosis?	Is there a contractual statement? Is the problem to be worked on delineated? Is a time frame indicated? Is a treatment plan outlined? Are goals clearly stated? Are goals appropriate to the person, the problem, and the setting?	Does activity follow the contract or plans? If not, does a subsequent note indicate reasons for the change? Was there appropriate communication with the referral source?	Does outcome statement indicate progress towards goals and status of any remaining relevant problems? Was closing appropriately timed?

39

TABLE 6. (*Continued*)

Program Number	Initial Contact	Assessment/Diagnosis	Treatment Plan/Goals	Service Delivery	Termination/Outcome

19	Is information identifying the client included?
	Is the date of the initial contact included?
		Does the social history include the following:
		a. Health–Medical:
		  1. Current functioning—activities of daily living
		  2. Adjustment to condition or illness
		b. Personal functioning:
		  1. Intellectual
		  2. Emotional
		  3. Social
		  4. Sexual
		  5. Cultural/religious
		c. Family/significant others:
		  1. Composition
		  2. Functioning
		  3. Support/protection system
		d. Environment:
		  1. Housing/living arrangements
		  2. Management of physical surroundings
		  3. Environmental barriers
			Are goals clearly indicated?
			Are plans clearly indicated?
			Are goals a result of problem identification and assessment?
			Is there a statement indicating the inclusion of client/significant others in the planning?
					Are outcomes stated?
					Is there an indication of the status of the plan's implementation?
					Is there an indication of the status of the goal's achievement?
					If the problem remains unresolved, why?

40

TABLE 6. (*Continued*)

Program Number	Initial Contact	Assessment/Diagnosis	Treatment Plan/Goals	Service Delivery	Termination/Outcome

		e. Economic:
		   1. Source of income
		   2. Money for daily needs
		   3. Money for medical needs
		   4. Money management
		 f. Educational/ vocational (school/work history)
		 g. Legal:
		   1. Rights
		   2. Protection
		   3. Guardianship/custody
		   4. Suspected abuse or neglect
		   5. Other legal matters
		
		 Are the problems clearly stated?
		 Is the client's perception of the problem stated?
		 Is the worker's assessment a result of a review of psychosocial problems?			

TABLE 6. (*Continued*)

Program Number	Initial Contact	Assessment/Diagnosis	Treatment Plan/Goals	Service Delivery	Termination/Outcome
14	Does the initial note state the following: a. Reason for referral b. Source of referral	Are the following noted: a. Patient's medical situation? b. Patient's perception of medical/social problem? c. A past history? d. Assessment of the current life situation? e. The family's or others' perception of the problem? f. Observable affect, defense, and mental status?	Social work plan: a. Is it clearly stated? b. Is it a direct response to the reason for referral? (If no, is there an explanation of the change of focus?)	Continuing social work intervention: a. Is it noted? b. Does it follow the initially stated plan? (If no, does the subsequent note indicate reasons for changes in the plan?)	Is there a discharge summary? Does it document the outcome of social work plan? Are there recommendations for further intervention?
6	Was social work response within two days of admission?	Summary of review of previous medical chart Summary of interview(s) with patient/family Summary of interview(s) with physician/nurse Statement of problems to include following: a. Assessment of social functioning prior to hospitalization	Clearly stated objective for each problem identified in the assessment Identification of potential resources and their availability/accessibility to patient Statement of one or more interventions that will enable the patient/family to reach the objectives	Was the plan developed to meet patient/family objectives implemented?	Is there an evaluation in the discharge summary notes?

TABLE 6. (*Continued*)

Program Number	Initial Contact	Assessment/Diagnosis	Treatment Plan/Goals	Service Delivery	Termination/Outcome
		b. Assessment of underlying conditions in cases of inpatient problem behavior c. Assessment of stress impact on patient and family d. Assessment of patient and family's acceptance of illness and capacity to utilize health resources			
18[b]	Is the date of the referral to social work services or the date of the initial contact stated? Is the source of referral or how the client got to social work services clearly stated? Should the referral source have been contacted? If yes, was the referral source contacted? Is the reason for referral (request for service) clearly stated?	Has the psychosocial information essential to this case been presented (e.g., demographic characteristics, family composition, economic status, living arrangements, patient's relationships, patient's perception of preventing problem, past history of the problem)? Is it understood whether the patient was previously known to the hospital division's social work department?	Are the goals stated? Were the goals mutually agreed on by worker and patient (or family)? If there is an assessment, do the goals follow logically from the assessment? Is there a treatment plan? Has the patient (or surrogate) been involved in the development of the treatment plan?	If there is a treatment plan, does the social work activity follow from the treatment plan? If involvement with the health care team was called for, does the social work activity indicate involvement with the team? If involvement with the patient's family was called for, does the social work activity indicate involvement with the family?	Is there a concluding note that summarizes the work between client and worker? Does the concluding note indicate progress made? Does the concluding note state whether the case was referred, transferred, or closed? Does the concluding note state why the case was referred, transferred, or closed?

43

TABLE 6. (*Continued*)

Program Number	Initial Contact	Assessment/Diagnosis	Treatment Plan/Goals	Service Delivery	Termination/Outcome
	Does the reason for referral or request for service fall within the realm of social work service?	Is it understood whether the patient was known to other agencies? Does the assessment indicate an integration of the psychosocial information? Does the assessment indicate an understanding of the psychosocial information? Are the patient's problems clearly stated? Are the problems related to the request for service or referral? If no, was an adequate explanation for the difference given? Are there potential problems that have not been noted or explained? Is it understood which problems will be the focus of social work intervention? Have the appropriate problems been selected for social work intervention?	Is the treatment plan sufficiently clear so that anyone picking up the case would be able to implement it? Have the aspects of the treatment plan that should be followed by other disciplines been identified?	Does the social work activity give the impression of thoughtful service? Does the social work activity give the impression of appropriate service?	Does the concluding note indicate whether there was a need for or a lack of need for follow-up? If there is a need for follow-up, are the follow-up plans appropriate? If there is a need for follow-up, were the follow-up plans carried out? Should this case have been terminated? Referred? Transferred? Continued for follow-up? Was the treatment plan implemented? Are the results indicated? If not implemented, are reasons given for why the plan was not implemented? Were the goals achieved?

[b] This list was substantially shortened for inclusion here.

44

TABLE 6. (*Continued*)

Program Number	Initial Contact	Assessment/Diagnosis	Treatment Plan/Goals	Service Delivery	Termination/Outcome
25	Is the source of referral stated? Is the patient's or informant's perception of problem stated?	Assessment should always include the following components: Statement identifying patient's personality type, i.e., what kind of person this is Statement describing how this personality is manifested Statement of patient's problem and its cause Statement explaining how the problem is behaviorally manifested Statement of attempts made by patient to resolve the problem Statement indicating what is needed to resolve the problem(s) Statement describing the patient's sick role or the patient's role adaptation	Is there a statement explaining what the worker intends to do about the problem(s)? (Give reference number in temporary problem list.) Is the plan consistent with the assessment?	Have the following statements been recorded: a. Statement describing what the worker did in relationship to the problem(s) (give reference number in temporary problem list)? b. Statement explaining what worker recommends that the patient do regarding the problem(s)? c. Statement indicating any referrals, either inter- or intra-hospital or to outside agencies?	

45

TABLE 6. (*Continued*)

Program Number	Initial Contact	Assessment/Diagnosis	Treatment Plan/Goals	Service Delivery	Termination/Outcome
		Statement describing the causal relationship between the health problem and any social, emotional, and psychological problem(s) Patient's demographic characteristics			
26	Is there documentation or referral?	Are the psychosocial problems listed? Is there a summary statement/assessment?	Is there an outline of the plan for the patient?	Is there documentation that patient has been informed of the situation and of aftercare alternatives? Are there current progress notes?	Is final case disposition noted?
27	Did the social worker respond promptly to the request for help?		Were patient and family involved in planning?	Did the social worker: Provide a service? Record any services on the chart? Make referrals to appropriate agencies? Keep the physician informed? Identify gaps in care? Seek alternatives if the desired goals were not attainable?	Were satisfactory solutions to problems achieved?

46

     1. The patient's physiological condition.
     2. The patient's psychological (cognitive, affective, and attitudinal) characteristics.
     3. The patient's environmental (social, cultural, legal, economic, familial, and physical) situation.
  c. This assessment should lead to the identification of the problems that are within the capacity and authority of the department.
  d. The patient's perception of the problems to be worked on should be noted.
3. Treatment plan/goal formulation
  a. The plans or goals for addressing the problems to be worked on should be specified.
  b. There should be evidence that the patient agrees with and/or understands these plans or goals.
4. Intervention
  a. The activities undertaken with and on behalf of the patient should be specified.
  b. These activities should be consistent with the original or modified plan for treatment or formulation of goals.
5. Termination/outcome
  a. The status of the client's problems or goals subsequent to intervention should be specified.
  b. Clients should achieve their goals and/or resolve the problems chosen for work.
  c. When goals are not achieved or problems resolved, reasons and other potential solutions should be specified.

Specific criteria. Peer review systems with sets of criteria developed for specific diseases, social problems, or social services were numerous. Sets of criteria were developed for the specific problem areas appearing in Table 7. It is impossible to present in this report all the specific sets of criteria developed as part of the systems reviewed. However, since several hospitals created criteria for the planning of posthospital care, some of these criteria are presented in Table 8.

The advantages of using social-problem or service-specific criteria are that they can be more precise and detailed than general criteria. This reduces errors in judgment and, therefore, increases validity and reliability. The precision of these criteria allows them to be applied by medical records analysts with clear directions of how to determine whether the criteria are met. This reduces costs and avoids using extensive amounts of professional time in conducting reviews.

TABLE 7. PROBLEMS FOR WHICH SPECIFIC CRITERIA HAVE BEEN DEVELOPED

Problem	Program Number
Discharge planning	1, 13, 7, 23, 21
Referral to home care	9, 12, 20
Referral to nursing home	12, 17, 26
Adjustment to illness	13, 17, 21
Social counseling	13
Psychosocial evaluation	13, 17, 21
Psychosocial functioning	13, 21
Facilitating services	13, 21
Interpersonal relationships	14, 17
Rheumatoid arthritis	7
Failure to thrive	7, 10
Cancer in children	7
Migraine headaches	7
Suspected child abuse	7, 17, 25
Severe burns	7
Respiratory failure	7
Obesity	7
Seizures	7
Adolescent pregnancy	7
Quadriplegia	7
Renal disease	7
Leukemia	7
Spinal cord injury	20
Hypertension	23
Pediatrics	23
Tubal ligation	10
Kidney transplant	10
Hip replacement	10
Myocardial infarction	10

The advantage of disease-specific and general-process criteria is that they can be used in interdisciplinary and multidisciplinary studies, in which topics are usually defined by a particular medical problem. This is likely to be more cost effective, since a single reviewer can examine a record using criteria from several disciplines. Such criteria also make it possible to examine the work of the total health team, and since everyone involved has an impact on the patient's well-being, it is often necessary to review the combined efforts to get a true picture of the quality of patient care.

TABLE 8. EXAMPLES OF PROBLEM-SPECIFIC CRITERIA: POSTHOSPITAL HOME CARE

Program 12	Programs 13 and 21	Program 20	Program 9
There must be a statement about referral in the chart.	The chart must contain the following:	There must be evidence of the following activities:	There must be evidence of the following circumstances:
There must be a statement in the chart reflecting how the patient is reacting to the illness/hospitalization.	Evidence that there was an assessment of the patient's social support system and medical situation (include source of information).	Consultation with ward personnel (physicians and/or nurses) regarding referral of a patient apparently suitable for home health care.	Patient plans to return home.
			Family or significant other(s) accept patient's plan to return home.
There must be a statement in the chart that shows how the patient is handling the situation.	Evidence of patient/family/significant-other participation.	Interview with patient and/or family concerning a description of home health care and to obtain consent for participation in the program.	Patient requires multiple services at home.
There must be a statement in the chart indicating that the social worker has evaluated the patient's personal relationships (relatives, neighbors, friends).	Evidence of collaboration with other hospital staff.		Direct patient care service not required twenty-four hours a day.
	A clear statement of the identified discharge problem.	Visiting Nurse Association referral made and documented:	Necessary equipment and supplies identified.
If community resources have been made available to the patient, the specific resource must be mentioned.	A clear statement of the plan including an appropriate follow-up.	1. Physician's order sheet signed (including date of the first appointment with the clinic).	Finances to support program are available.
There must be a statement in the chart indicating whether the case will be closed or followed, and a plan must be stated.	Evidence of responsiveness to continuing communication regarding the patient's needs among the social worker, patient, family, and practitioners from other disciplines.	2. Staff report sheet of supportive service activities, which must include social service description of home situation.	Date the social worker referred patient to organized home care must be recorded.
	Evidence of implementation of the plan.	3. Discharge planner sheet.	Patient accepted for organized home care.

TABLE 8. *(Continued)*

Program 12	Programs 13 and 21	Program 20	Program 9
		Obtaining of necessary prostheses, appliances, and sick room supplies.	
		Arrangements for suitable transportation upon patient's discharge.	
		Observation of written nurse progress report within two weeks after discharge and regularly thereafter.	
		Documentation of home visits by social worker if requested by visiting nurse.	
		Documentation of first clinic visit following discharge.	
		Transfer of social service information to outpatient record.	
		Documentation of multidisciplinary case conferences as indicated.	
		Documentation of ongoing social service coordinator.	
		Readmission to hospital on priority basis if advised by visiting nurse.	

50

GUARANTEED ACCESS SYSTEMS

Quality assurance programs also include, as a third component, procedures to assure that hospital patients who need social work services are actually receiving them. This component focuses on the total patient population, rather than only on those who are actually seen by a social worker. It frequently contains a set of patient characteristics that are believed to indicate a high probability that social work services will be needed. This set of characteristics can be used in several ways. It can be part of a concurrent or utilization review in the hospital. When a patient who has one of these characteristics is found to lack documentation of social work involvement, either the attending physician or the social work department is notified. Another approach is to include these indicators in the retrospective reviews that medical records analysts conducted on specific types of cases. Indicators for social work involvement are used as criteria. Those cases for which social work is indicated but not received are then judged unacceptable.

Ten systems reviewed had developed access criteria, and these criteria were in different states of implementation. Some were used only as guidelines for social work and other hospital personnel. Others were incorporated in concurrent or retrospective review criteria or used in screening or automatic referral procedures. Most programs had developed criteria to be applied to all types of patients, although a few had a different set of criteria for each age group or each division of the hospital. Some examples of general access criteria appear in Table 9.

RELATIONSHIPS AMONG COMPONENTS

Only seven of the programs examined had all three components in operation—the information, peer review, and guaranteed access systems. In these programs the three components were interrelated in various ways. Findings from the information system, for example, affected aspects of peer review. Norms of patient care and studies of patients' characteristics were used to develop criteria for peer review, and studies of client outcome and activities of workers suggested areas needing in-depth examination through peer review. Findings from

51

TABLE 9. EXAMPLES OF CRITERIA FOR SOCIAL WORK ACCESS

Program 14
- All cancer patients
- All open heart surgeries
- All head and spinal cord injuries
- All stroke patients
- All patients with no identifying information
- All patients over age 60 with no relatives living at the same address

Program 12
- Accident victims
- The aged
- The chronic or terminally ill
- Frightened, withdrawn children
- Abused or neglected children
- Newborns who are premature or with birth anomalies
- Suicidal or asserted adults
- Disabling or disfiguring conditions
- Abortions, vasectomies, unmarried pregnancies
- Psychosomatic conditions
- Frequent users of emergency room
- Marital or family problems

Program 6
- Any patient over age 62 who lives alone or with an invalid.
- Suspected child abuse and neglect of patient under age 18.
- Out-of-town patient who will need to remain in or return frequently to this area for outpatient cobalt or radiation treatment.
- Patient with no relative and who is unable to give information at time of admission.
- Patient transferred to hospital from a nursing or foster home.
- Chronically ill patient on rehospitalization.
- Patient with a condition likely to cause increasing impairment.
- Adult patient unable to care for himself.
- Patient who may need special equipment at home.
- Obstetrical patient in the following situations:

Program 5

Automatic referral:
- Over age 70, living alone, eye surgery projected.
- Institutional transfer into hospital

High risk:
- Eighty years old and over
- Seventy years old and over, living alone
- Emergency admission (except appendicitis, hernias, pneumonias)
- Severe, life-threatening illness (i.e., metastatic or germinal cancer and blood syscrasins)
- Illness involving severe physical dysfunctioning (i.e., organic and/or mental brain syndrome, encephalopathies; syrongomyelin, cardiovascular accident and stroke, aphasia, pathological fractures; carcinoma of the colon, rectum, pancreas, brain, or masses leading to "ostomies";

Program 20
- Cerebral vascular accident
- Cancer
- Cardiac
- Diabetes
- Brain damage
- Neurosurgery
- Amputations
- Disfiguring surgery
- Burn
- Prematures
- Birth anomalies
- Patients requesting abortions
- Child abuse
- Rape
- Lead poisoning
- Psychiatric
- Homeless
- Uncooperative patient
- Prosthesis or appliance candidates

Programs 13 and 21
- Patient admitted from a nursing home, chronic care facility, or foster home.
- Patient whose condition might affect his ability to return home.
- Patient with no known family or adequate social and financial support systems.
- Patient with a history of frequent readmission or hospitalization within one year.
- Patient exhibiting prolonged fear and/or anxiety about recommended medical procedures.
- Patient who is a suspected victim of abuse, neglect, or violence.
- Patient with identified problems whose medical compliance hinges on adequate housing and/or physical conditions.
- Patient whose condition will necessitate a change in education, employment, and/or family role.

Table 9. (Continued)

Program 12	Program 6	Program 5	Program 20	Programs 13 and 21
Financial problems	Management problems	any limb surgery leading to amputation as a result of diabetes, gangrene, circulatory diseases; carcinoma of the throat, vocal chord, larynx, tongue, airway obstructions leading to "ec-tomies"; renal diseases leading to dialysis and/or transplant; multiple fractures; eye disorders that are sight threatening, such as glaucoma and retinal detachment).		Patient whose condition has resulted in identified problems which will negatively affect self-image, appearance, or physical and/or sexual functioning.
	1. Adoption is requested.			Patient whose identified family problems directly affect care, treatment, and medical compliance.
	2. Out-of-town patient with complicated pregnancy or delivery.			Patient or patient's family exhibiting behavior that is disruptive to treatment.
	3. Patient is mentally retarded.	Chronic diseases (i.e., lupus, Hodgkins, myasthenia gravida, ulcerative colitis, multiple sclerosis, cerebral palsy, hemophilia, sickle cell, muscular dystrophy, rheumatoid arthritis, liver diseases).		Patient who is a nonresident of this state and has an illness which will affect his or her ability to return home.
	If a social worker from another agency is named in the chart.			Patient admitted for treatment as a result of a catastrophic event.
				Patient in the terminal stages of illness.
				Patient whose hospitalization and/or medical compliance depends on specific supports in the home.

the guaranteed access system often suggested areas needing in-depth study. Both the information system and the access insurance system produced findings suggesting corrective action, which sometimes involved making changes in the information system or the access system. Some of the relationships among the three components are schematically represented in Table 10.

Costs of Programs

The costs of quality assurance can be divided into those related to program development and those related to the operation of the program. Few respondents were able to estimate all their costs for quality assurance, but most reported that funds for this function came from departmental operating budgets. In addition, two programs received funds from professional organizations (Programs 3 and 8), two used federal funds (Programs 6 and 22), and one benefited greatly from contributed time by a systems analyst (Program 17).

The biggest cost element in program development was in the time of social workers. This time was usually spent in committee meetings to develop criteria for peer review or to identify data elements for an information system. It was impossible to estimate the benefits of participating in this process, but many reported that it resulted both in learning about quality assurance and in developing a commitment to it. Systems requiring special computer programs also had the writing and implementation of the program as a major cost element. Cost estimates ranged from $500 for a small list of peer review criteria to $100,000 for a complex, extensively tested program that included an automated information system, peer review, and access analysis.

The second group of costs was associated with the ongoing operation of the program. Peer review included costs for personnel to conduct record reviews, examine exceptions, produce reports, and plan and undertake corrective action. Information systems involved expenditures for social work time to complete the necessary forms, as well as costs for key punching, computer time and operation, and the social work interpretation of output.

Accurate estimates of these operational costs were again

TABLE 10. EXAMPLES OF RELATIONSHIPS AMONG COMPONENTS

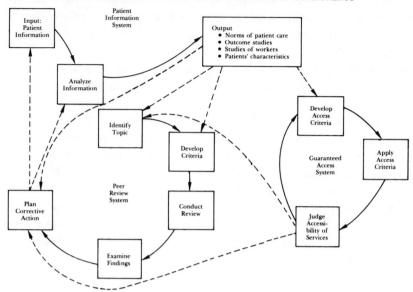

difficult to obtain. However, computer programs for information systems differed in their efficiency; systems yielding similar outputs had wide differences in costs. One of the biggest costs in peer review was for social work personnel. The peer review system that required social workers to make judgments about whether practice was appropriate or adequate on a number of criteria were especially costly. Peer review systems whose criteria could initially be applied by medical records analysts or other trained reviewers were much less costly.

Use of Findings

The findings produced by these quality assurance programs were found to be useful in several ways. Informants reported that the findings were most frequently used for improving social work practice through in-service training and continuing education. The next most frequent use was for guiding management and personnel decisions.

Almost all respondents reported that their programs were associated with improvements in worker performance and recording. These judgments were based almost exclusively on impressions. Workers were seen as becoming more aware of their own practice and more goal oriented. Some became better organized and used their time more efficiently. The peer review process resulted in the sharing of practice-related information, and recording became more timely, complete, and uniform.

Respondents also reported that, as a result of quality assurance activities, the role of the social worker in the hospital became clearer to both social workers and other professionals. This occurred in multidisciplinary reviews and also resulted from improved communication through better recording. There was only one report of evidence that the quality assurance program had affected patients (Program 2), but no one believed that it had, in any case, been detrimental to care.

Summary

This study examined twenty-seven social work quality assurance programs in varying stages of development. The programs tended to have developed mainly in the larger teaching hospitals in the Northeast and Midwest, although small hospitals and other regions were represented.

The most comprehensive programs consisted of three interrelated components:

Patient information systems designed to gather and analyze information on patient characteristics, problems, services received, and outcomes of service.

Peer review systems designed to compare the actual social work care delivered to patients with a set of criteria for adequate care.

Guaranteed access systems designed to increase the probability that patients able to benefit from social work services will actually receive them.

The findings from the analyses of information-system data were used to guide the creation of peer review criteria, and they contributed to access insurance by identifying indicators of the need for social work service. Further, the data from information systems were analyzed to answer evaluative questions about social work practice and to assist in management decisions.

Findings from peer review led to the identification of inadequate practice throughout entire departments or among certain workers with certain types of patients. Access insurance contributed to the identification of groups of patients likely to lack access to service. Ideally, when findings revealed inadequacies in social work practice or access, corrective action was instituted. Similarly, when the quality assurance program yielded new knowledge about social work practice, this knowledge was disseminated.

The components of social work quality assurance programs had direct applicability to some hospital PSRO programs. Some concurrent review systems incorporated indicators of the need for social work service. In some places, social work peer review criteria were incorporated into multidisciplinary reviews. Retrospective studies of social work care using data either from the information system or from a peer review system at times served as medical care evaluation studies (but not as JCAH audits). Finally, profile analyses of social work patients were produced from information systems.

5
ISSUES, RECOMMENDATIONS, AND FUTURE DIRECTIONS

The preceding analysis of quality assurance programs can be used in several ways. First, it can provide specific examples of approaches to quality assurance that may be selected or modified for use in other facilities. Second, it raises a series of issues and questions that must be studied, debated, and resolved as quality assurance programs evolve. Finally, the instances of consensus the analysis uncovered among independently developed programs can be used to recommend some uniform standards for quality assurance programs in social work. This chapter will discuss both the issues the report raises and the standards it suggests.

Issues

Several general issues need careful consideration. Two of the most important are the validity of program components and the program costs. Persons involved in the development of quality assurance programs must remain mindful of these issues.

VALIDITY

The validity of a quality assurance program depends on two important elements: (1) the extent to which the aspects of care examined are actually indicators of good care, and (2) the extent to which the aspects of care examined are accurately assessed or measured, that is, the reliability of the data produced by the information system. The ultimate validation of any criteria of quality is that care complying with these criteria is more beneficial to patients than care that does not comply with them. When patient outcome is an indicator of quality, the criteria set must focus on results that are desirable. For example, adequate health, improved social functioning, and reduction of problems and distress are among the kinds of outcomes that may be considered desirable. Further, the procedures used to measure the extent to which these desirable outcomes have been achieved must be reliable, that is, free of error.

When client outcomes are used as indicators of quality, it is difficult to know whether these outcomes are a product of social work service. For example, if a certain level of goal attainment is selected as a criterion for acceptable client outcome, we cannot, in the absence of a comparison group receiving no social work services, know whether it was the social work service that caused the outcome. Similarly, if patients did not reach an acceptable goal level, we will not know whether they would have deteriorated without social work service.[1]

The problems of validity are slightly different when the focus of the quality assurance program is on social work structure or process. To be valid, criteria for social work structure or process must be related to the occurrence of desirable results. For example, if a certain level of staff training is one structural criterion, the level of training set as a minimal criterion must lead to a greater probability of desirable client outcomes than would a lower level of training. If training makes no difference in the care of patients, the criterion is not valid.

Similarly, the validity of the criteria selected for the process of service depends for the most part on whether compliance with the criteria produces better results for patients than noncompliance. Process criteria that result in administrative efficiency may also be valid for that purpose. For example, suppose a system calls for a judgment of whether the psycho-

---

[1] The certainty about the effects of intervention can be increased through the use of single-subject research designs. *See,* for example, Michael Hersen and David Barlow, *Single Case Experimental Designs* (New York: Pergamon Press, 1976); and Michael Howe, "Casework Self-Evaluation: A Single-Subject Approach," *Social Service Review,* 48 (January 1974), pp. 1–23.

social history obtained was adequate. It should follow that the probability of achieving a desired outcome is greater for those patients whose history is judged to be adequate than for those whose history is judged to be inadequate. It should be noted that several elements of practice will probably interact to produce the desired outcomes. Therefore, it is more realistic to suggest that an entire set of criteria is valid if compliance with them is related to desirable outcomes.

Moreover, even if the structural or process criteria selected are related to desired outcomes, these criteria must be accurately measured. For example, several judges rating the adequacy of a social history should agree. Similarly, the same record reviewed several times should receive the same judgment on its compliance with the criteria.

Another group of criteria are those set for insuring access, that is, criteria applied to a total patient population to see whether those people possibly needing social work services actually receive them. These criteria are valid to the extent that they identify patients who are likely to benefit from receiving service. In other words, the criteria should not result in patients being identified as needing service if an assessment reveals that they do not need service (that is, false positives). Nor are criteria valid if too many patients needing service are omitted (that is, false negatives). How many false positives and negatives can be tolerated depends on the costs of seeing the false positives compared to the consequences for the false negatives of not receiving service. Further, since patients needing service become known to social work in several ways in addition to the application of access criteria, criteria are cost effective when they identify individuals who need service but whom those other mechanisms overlook.

COSTS

A second major issue in developing quality assurance programs is their cost and feasibility. It has been difficult to estimate the costs of quality assurance programs, since they usually develop over a long period and are funded from departmental operating budgets. Further, some components of quality assurance have replaced previous recording procedures and statistical reporting and have thus eliminated these costs. Peer review has supplemented traditional supervision and may, therefore, have decreased this cost. In addition, the many reportedly beneficial effects of quality assurance activities on the knowledge and performance of workers must be kept in mind when considering costs.

There is some evidence that peer review systems that use medical records analysts for the initial application of criteria to the medical record are less costly than those that need social workers to conduct the chart reviews. The systems that require social workers to make professional judgments about the adequacy or appropriateness of numerous aspects of practice have the highest personnel costs. However, this cost differential must be compared with the benefits that may accrue to social workers as a result of their involvement in the actual review.

Information systems are less costly when the forms used for data collection are also useful for recording information relevant to practice. To be cost effective, each data element collected should be necessary for answering practice or management questions. The routine collection of large amounts of data that are not used for evaluating practice, building knowledge, or making management decisions is wasteful. It is more cost effective to create information systems that are flexible enough to permit the collection of special data on a time-limited, sample basis. After the specific questions are answered, the collection of these special data elements may be discontinued.

Computer programming is another major cost in information systems, especially during the development of a system when reporting formats and data elements must be changed repeatedly. One way to avoid this cost is to rely on available statistical packages to provide analysis in the early stages of developing the system. When the data elements and reporting procedures have been tested and stabilized, a permanent program can be written to generate the desired reports.

Recommendations

In view of the issues related to the validity and effectiveness of quality assurance programs, it is desirable that the social work profession move toward uniformity in its approach to quality assurance. The need is for some basic principles that can guide the establishment of quality assurance programs around the country. These principles must be general enough that they are applicable in a variety of settings, yet specific enough to produce a minimum level of similarity among quality assurance programs in social work.

One technique for identifying such principles is to look for areas of agreement in existing quality assurance programs. The consensual approach to generating principles or standards is based on several assumptions. First, it assumes that when independent groups have developed similar structure or content in quality assurance programs, this reflects a significant consensus. Second, it assumes that when there is significant consensus about the structure and content of programs, this represents desirable structure and content for quality assurance programs. Third, it assumes that quality assurance programs which employ the principles or standards identified by consensus are more likely to contribute to effective and efficient service delivery than those that do not follow those principles.

Under these assumptions, the preceding study can be used to identify areas in which there is agreement on the necessary ingredients and operation of quality assurance programs. These areas of agreement can then constitute principles or standards that should guide social workers when they implement quality assurance programs in their own settings. A series of such recommendations follows.

RECOMMENDED COMPONENTS

In general, all hospital social work departments in health care facilities should have their own quality assurance programs or participate in regional quality assurance programs. A quality assurance program must systematically evaluate patient-related aspects of social work practice and take action to correct any observed deficiencies.

Quality assurance programs should eventually contain, at a minimum, the following interrelated components:

A patient/provider information system. This is an ongoing mechanism for collecting, storing, and analyzing patient-related information.

A peer review system. This is a set of procedures by which a group of professional peers evaluate the quality of care delivered to patients and determine when corrective action is needed.

A guaranteed access system. This is a mechanism for assuring that patients who need social work services are actually receiving them.

Information systems should have the capacity to collect and store data on provider and patient inputs, outputs, and outcomes. At a minimum, the following data elements should be included for each patient:

Patient's characteristics. These are the relevant physical, social, psychological, and demographic characteristics of the patient.

Patient's problems. This is the assignment of the patient's problems to meaningful categories.

Services received. These are the categories of activities engaged in by the social worker on behalf of the patient.

Patient outcomes. This is a measurement of the patient's status subsequent to receiving social work service (that is, the extent to which desired results have been achieved).

These data should be analyzed to answer at least the following questions: Are desirable results for patients being achieved? For what types of patients, with what kinds of problems, receiving what kinds of services are these results being achieved? Answers to these questions should be used both to evaluate practice and to establish norms to be used in peer review.

Peer review systems should, at a minimum, examine the process of practice in the following areas:

1. Initial contact
   a. The initial contact with the patient should be timely.
   b. Early collaboration should occur with the referral source.
   c. Some judgment of the appropriateness of a case for social work service should be made.
2. Assessment/diagnosis
   a. A psychosocial assessment should be reported for every patient.
   b. Several areas of functioning should be included in the assessment, such as these:

1. The patient's physiological condition.
2. The patient's psychological characteristics—cognitive, affective, and attitudinal.
3. The patient's environmental situation—social, cultural, legal, economic, familial, and physical.
   c. This assessment should lead to the selection of problems to be worked on that are within the capacity and authority of the department.
   d. The patient's perception of the problems to be worked on should be noted.
3. Treatment plan/goal formulation
   a. The plans or goals for addressing the problems to be worked on should be specified.
   b. There should be evidence that the patient agrees with and/or understands these plans or goals.
4. Intervention
   a. The activities undertaken with and on behalf of the patient should be specified.
   b. These activities should be logically related to the original or modified treatment plan or goal formulation.
5. Termination/outcome
   a. The status of patients' problems or goals subsequent to service should be specified.
   b. Patients should achieve their goals and/or resolve their "problems to be worked on."
   c. In cases in which goals are not achieved or problems resolved, reasons and other potential solutions should be specified.

Guaranteed access systems should consist of indicators of the need for social work assessment that are applied to an entire patient population. This process should result in social work contact with those patients who are likely to need service according to the indicators. Age, living arrangements, and the severity or chronicity of the disease are among the areas in which indicators should be specified.

RECOMMENDED RELATIONSHIP TO PSRO

As mentioned earlier, quality assurance was a social work activity long before the passage of the PSRO legislation, and PSRO is just one of several influences on quality assurance programs. Further, social work quality assurance programs are designed mainly to improve the effectiveness and efficiency of social work services, rather than to comply with PSRO requirements. However, PSRO activities should be a meeting point for the quality assurance activities of social work and other disciplines.

Quality assurance activities in social work should relate to hospital PSRO activities in several ways. First, criteria for social work involvement (guaranteed access) should be incorporated into concurrent review. Thus, cases would be examined to determine whether those who, according to the criteria, should have been seen by a social worker were actually seen. Negative findings should result in corrective action.

Second, retrospective studies of social work services, either for specific patient groups or for a sample of a general patient population, should serve as medical care evaluation (MCE) studies.[2] In addition, social workers should participate in multidisciplinary or interdisciplinary MCEs in which social work process criteria are combined with criteria for other disciplines or in which social workers participate in developing a set of criteria for interdisciplinary team care.

Finally, social work information systems should produce profiles of patients. These profiles should complement the profile analyses performed on other hospital data sets and lead to the identification of MCE topics.

RECOMMENDED USE OF FINDINGS

The findings from quality assurance programs should be used to improve social work practice. Information systems that collect data on patients' characteristics, problems, services, and outcomes should be used to answer questions about social work practice. They have the capacity to contribute to building knowledge about which interventions are effective under what circumstances. They should compare workers on patterns of practice and suggest areas needing in-depth evaluation. They

---

[2] JCAH presently does not accept audits conducted solely on nonphysician services; audits of nonphysician services must be part of a multidisciplinary review that includes physician services.

should guide management decisions in the distribution of manpower and other resources.

Peer review systems should answer questions about whether practice in the setting tends to comply with what is acceptable practice. When deficiencies are observed, these findings should result in in-service training, continuing education, or personnel actions.

Finally, concurrent review of social work access should answer questions about whether social work services are reaching the population in need. If not, the findings should lead to procedures, such as routine screening or education of other personnel, which will insure that the patients who need services actually receive them.

The entire quality assurance program should contribute to the accountability of a social work program both to consumers and to the profession. This will occur if the criteria are valid in terms of consumer goals. In other words, if the program judges high-quality care as that which contributes to the well-being of the people it serves, it will satisfy both consumer and professional accountability.

RECOMMENDED PROFESSIONAL ACTIVITIES

The study also revealed areas of quality assurance programs in which there is no clear agreement. These are areas requiring immediate attention because uniformity is essential to making findings comparable and cumulative across settings.[3]

The first area needing attention is the classification of problems. The profession needs a uniform taxonomy of patients' problems. A recommended taxonomy for classifying patients' problems must contain categories that are exhaustive and mutually exclusive. It should contain sufficient categories so problems with different implications for practice are not lumped together. It should not, however, contain so many categories as to increase unreliability among workers making judgments about which category a problem really belongs to. Furthermore, too many categories result in too few patients in

---

[3] Beginning work in several of these areas has been undertaken by the Society for Hospital Social Work Directors of the American Hospital Association, Committee on Uniform Reporting.

66

some categories, making meaningful analysis difficult. A problem taxonomy should also reflect only the problem of the patient and exclude the service designed to alleviate that problem. Any recommended taxonomy must define each category precisely to minimize errors in its utilization. The taxonomy should be thoroughly field tested to determine its reliability and usefulness before its use is recommended on an ongoing basis.

A second area requiring work is the development of a uniform service classification.[4] A taxonomy for classifying services needs to be developed that meets the same requirements of mutual exclusivity, exhaustiveness, and reliability mentioned in the discussion of the problem taxonomy. The major difficulty to be resolved in classifying services is the determination of what should actually be categorized. Should the profession categorize activities workers perform, such as assessment, referral, and counseling? Or should it categorize packages of activities that constitute goal-oriented services, such as discharge planning and activities that facilitate family adjustment to illness? The important point is that these two levels of analysis should not be mixed in the same taxonomy.

A third area that requires attention is patient outcome, which needs a uniform approach to measuring the status of patients subsequent to service. However, such measurement requires extensive development and testing. A first step should be to develop some agreed on conceptualization of desirable outcomes. These expected results must be clearly specified so that they can guide the search for those characteristics of patients that should be measured in estimating whether desirable results were achieved. The resolution of problems seems to be the most commonly used concept at this point. Although such a concept has face validity, it produces many problems in comparing patients and facilities.[5] These and other difficulties must be addressed in any effort to create a uniform approach to measuring patient outcomes.

---

[4] The U.S. Department of Health, Education, and Welfare is sponsoring efforts to create a service taxonomy that would be acceptable to public and private human service organizations.

[5] For a discussion of these issues, see Claudia Coulton and Phyllis Solomon, "Measuring Outcomes of Intervention," Social Work Research and Abstracts, 13 (Winter 1977), pp. 3–9.

A final area needing immediate work is the development of a uniform set of patients' characteristics for quality assurance. This set of characteristics should reflect the minimum information needed to understand and interpret findings about patients' problems, services, and outcomes. Nonessential data elements should be optional, depending on the resources and special interests of each facility. The units for coding each characteristic should be clearly specified and field tested for reliability. Progress has already been made in this area through the work of the Committee on Uniform Reporting of the Society for Hospital Social Work Directors of the American Hospital Association.

All the areas of quality assurance on which there is not clear agreement should be addressed by a national-level committee made up of social work practitioners, administrators, and researchers with experience in health care. To facilitate the formulation of uniform approaches, the committee should establish procedures for ongoing communication with practitioners in the field. This will be necessary because quality assurance programs are in an evolutionary phase, and the recommendations, guidelines, and standards for these programs must also evolve gradually and be revised as the principles are tested and new approaches tried.

Future Directions

There are some additional trends that will probably affect social work quality assurance programs in the more distant future and for which the profession should begin to prepare. First, it is likely that there will be increased impetus toward multidisciplinary and interdisciplinary reviews. This is the direction both JCAH and PSRO are promoting. It is most consistent with the concept of a health care team in which several professions simultaneously apply their skills to produce the best possible results for the patient. Further, such reviews are more cost effective, since the patient's chart can be reviewed a single time for several professions. Such multidisciplinary reviews will probably require that social work develop sets of criteria that are applicable to the medically defined problems usually selected for review by multidisciplinary groups. These criteria must also be precise enough to be applied by medical records analysts.

Second, it is probable that the data from social work information systems will be used in multivariate analyses to build knowledge about social work practice. There is increasing concern about training social work practitioners to provide effective services to people with health problems. Such training will be facilitated by the formulation of an empirically validated set of practice principles.

Third, there will probably be an increasing tendency for peer review to focus on outcome in addition to process. Efforts will be made to determine whether process criteria are valid by examining whether they lead to desirable outcomes. When process criteria are thus validated, there will be a tendency to return to the use of these criteria because they are usually easier and less costly to apply.

Fourth, social work departments will increasingly incorporate their quality assurance activities into departmental operations. Some traditional record-keeping tasks will be replaced by procedures developed for quality assurance. Some supervisory activities will be performed through peer review. Management decisions will also be facilitated by quality assurance findings.

Finally, there will be attempts to add cost data to the information systems and to relate these data to high-quality care in process, outcome, and access. The costs of quality assurance activities will also be examined to determine whether certain approaches achieve the same degree of accountability for less cost than others.

APPENDIX A

Interview Schedule for
Quality Assurance Programs

1. Please briefly describe the major components of your quality assurance system.

_____

_____

_____

_____

_____

_____

_____

Setting

The questions in this section pertain to the setting in which you have used this system.

2. In which type of setting has this system been tested?
   1. General hospital, community ☐
   2. General hospital, teaching ☐
   3. Psychiatric hospital ☐
   4. Pediatric hospital ☐
   5. Governmental hospital ☐
   6. Other, specialized hospital ☐
   7. Long-term care facility ☐
   8. Ambulatory care facility ☐
   9. Other (Please specify.) ☐

71

3. What is the size of the setting in which this system has been tested?
   1. No beds ☐
   2. 1–250 beds ☐
   3. 251–500 beds ☐
   4. 501–750 beds ☐
   5. 751–1,000 beds ☐
   6. More than 1,001 beds ☐
4. Does this setting provide ambulatory care?
   1. Yes ☐
   2. No ☐
5. What is the size of the social work staff in the setting in which this system has been tested?
   A. Number of DSWs/Ph.D.'s _____
   B. Number of MSWs _____
   C. Number of BSWs _____
   D. Number of aides _____
6. What is the average number of new social work service cases per month?
   A. Inpatient _____
   B. Outpatient _____

Definitions

7. People seem to have different meanings for terms they use in quality assurance. Tell how you and/or those who worked on this system defined the following terms:
   A. Quality Assurance: _____
   _____
   _____
   _____
   _____

   B. Peer Review: _____
   _____
   _____
   _____
   _____

   C. Audit: _____
   _____
   _____
   _____
   _____

D. Criteria: _____

_____

_____

_____

_____

E. Norms: _____

_____

_____

_____

_____

F. Standards: _____

_____

_____

_____

_____

Development

The questions that follow pertain to the events and activities that led up to your quality assurance system.

8. Please rank the following objectives according to their importance as objectives of your system: (Assign 1 to the most important objective, 2 to the second most important objective, and so on; assign 8 to the least important objective.)

	Objective	*Rank*
a.	To comply with PSRO requirements.	_____
b.	To obtain information to justify social work services to hospital administration.	_____
c.	To assure that social workers delivered appropriate services.	_____
d.	To build knowledge about social work in health care.	_____
e.	To obtain information for management decisions.	_____
f.	To evaluate the effectiveness of social work services.	_____
g.	To measure the efficiency of social work services.	_____
h.	Other (Please specify.) _____	

9. When did work begin on the development of this system?

　　　　———————　　　　　　———————
　　　　　Month　　　　　　　　　Year

10. Was this system developed primarily in your facility or as part of an effort of social workers from several facilities?
　　1. In this facility　　　　　　　　　　　□
　　2. With social workers from other facilities　□

If you checked "1," go on to A and skip B. If you checked "2," skip A and go on to B.

A. If the system was developed in your facility who participated? Check all that apply.
　　a. Social work staff　　　　　　　　　□
　　b. Consumers　　　　　　　　　　　　□
　　c. Medical records staff　　　　　　　□
　　d. Data processing staff　　　　　　　□
　　e. Medical staff　　　　　　　　　　□
　　f. Nursing staff　　　　　　　　　　□
　　g. Administrative staff　　　　　　　□
　　h. Outside consultants
　　　　(Please specify type.)　　　　　　□

　　　———————————————————————————————

B. If the system was developed with social workers from other facilities, who participated? (Check all that apply.)
　　a. Hospital social work directors　　　□
　　b. Hospital social work staff　　　　　□
　　c. Consumers　　　　　　　　　　　□
　　d. Social work researchers　　　　　　□
　　e. Others (Please specify.)　　　　　□

　　　———————————————————————————————

11. The criteria developed were based on the following: (Check all that apply.)
　　a. Consensus of social workers　　　　□
　　b. Data collected on actual social work activities　□
　　c. Social work research　　　　　　　□
　　d. Social work practice literature　　　□
　　e. Other (Please specify.)　　　　　　□

　　　———————————————————————————————

12. Please estimate the costs of developing this system.
    Personnel
        Directors   ＿＿hours at $20/hr. ＿＿＿
        Staff   ＿＿hours at $15/hr. ＿＿＿
        Others   ＿＿hours at $ /hr. ＿＿＿
    Consultants (Specify type.)

    ＿＿＿＿＿＿＿＿＿＿＿＿＿   ＿＿＿

    ＿＿＿＿＿＿＿＿＿＿＿＿＿   ＿＿＿

    Electronic data processing   ＿＿＿
    Other (Please specify.)

    ＿＿＿＿＿＿＿＿＿＿＿＿＿   ＿＿＿

                        Total $＿＿＿

13. What sources of funds were used for developmental activities? (Check all that apply.)
    a. Departmental operating budget ☐
    b. Funds from professional organizations ☐
    c. Funds from local PSRO ☐
    d. Federal grant ☐
    e. Grant from other source ☐
    f. Volunteers whose time no one paid for ☐
    g. Other (Please specify.)

    ＿＿＿＿＿＿＿＿＿＿＿＿＿＿＿＿＿＿＿＿＿＿＿

14. What stage of development has your system reached?
    1. Just beginning to develop, never tested. ☐
    2. Initial testing and revision under way. ☐
    3. Testing and revision completed, now being implemented on a pilot basis. ☐
    4. Fully implemented in a few areas. ☐
    5. Fully implemented in many areas. Results are being used on an ongoing basis. ☐

Administration

Questions in this section address the mechanics of the actual or proposed implementation of your system.

15. Which unit in your hospital has overall responsibility for the operation of this system?
    1. Social work services ☐
    2. Medical records ☐
    3. Other (Please specify.) ☐

    ＿＿＿＿＿＿＿＿＿＿＿＿＿＿＿＿＿＿＿＿＿＿＿

16. What types of personnel are involved in the operation of the system? (Check all that apply.)
    a. Social workers ☐
    b. Medical records analysts ☐
    c. Clerical staff ☐
    d. Researchers ☐
    e. Key punchers ☐
    f. Coders ☐
    g. Computer programmers ☐
    h. Other (Please specify.) ☐

    _____

17. Is this system incorporated into the PSRO activities of your hospital?
    1. Yes ☐
    2. No ☐
    If yes,
       A. Is it used as a part of the following: (Check all that apply.)
          a. Concurrent review ☐
          b. Medical care evaluation study ☐
          c. Profile analysis ☐
          d. Other (Please specify.) ☐

    _____

18. What are the actual or estimated monthly costs of operating this system?
    Personnel
       Social workers _____
       Medical records analysts _____
       Data processing staff _____
       Clerical staff _____
       Researchers _____
       Others _____
    Consultants _____
    Materials _____
    Data processing _____
       Total $_____

19. What is the average number of cases reviewed each month? _____

20. How often are reviews conducted? _____

Characteristics of the System

This section pertains to the actual content of your system including sampling and data collection procedures, measurement of variables, and the instruments used.

21. What population of patients is reviewed by your system?
    A. Does it review the following:
       1. Inpatients □
       2. Outpatients □
       3. Both □
    B. Does it review the following:
       1. A total patient group □
       2. Only patients who receive social service □
    C. Does it review the following:
       1. Only Medicare, Medicaid, and Title V patients □
       2. All patients □

22. How are cases selected for review?
    1. All cases are included. □
    2. A random sample is selected. □
    3. A sample is selected by another procedure. (Please specify.) □
    _____
    _____

23. What is the source of data for your review? (Check all that apply.)
    a. Medical record □
    b. Social service record □
    c. Special form completed by worker □
    d. Special form completed by client □
    e. Other (Please specify.) □
    _____

24. What is the primary format used in your setting for social work recording in the medical record? (Choose one.)
    1. Problem-oriented medical record □
    2. Progress notes □
    3. Consultation form □
    4. Other (Please specify.) □
    _____

25. Does your system contain
    1. A single set of criteria applicable to all patients. ☐
    2. Separate set(s) of criteria for specific groups of
       patients. ☐
    If you checked 2, are the criteria grouped according to
    the following?
    1. Medical diagnosis ☐
    2. Psychosocial problem ☐
    3. Type of social work service provided ☐
    4. Other (Please specify.) ☐

26. Which of the following statements more closely resembles
    an assumption on which your system is based? (Choose
    one.)
    1. Professional social workers can develop valid
       criteria for practice. These criteria can be used
       to judge the quality of service based on a de-
       scription of what the worker did. ☐
    2. For the most part, social workers cannot say
       what interventions will produce desired out-
       comes. Therefore, to judge quality, we must
       look at whether desirable client outcomes were
       achieved after service. ☐

27. Which of the following best characterizes the major focus
    of your system? (Check one.)
    1. This system looks to see whether workers have
       recorded certain actions or pieces of informa-
       tion that are believed to be necessary for an
       acceptable quality of service. ☐
    2. This system reviews the social worker's record-
       ing and makes a judgment about the quality of
       the service he or she delivered to a particular
       patient. ☐
    3. This system examines client outcomes to deter-
       mine whether certain objectives were achieved. ☐
    4. This system collects data on clients' problems,
       interventions by workers, and/or client out-
       comes to be analyzed to determine the effec-
       tiveness of service. ☐
    5. This system collects information on the satisfac-
       tion of clients with social work service. ☐

If you checked responses 1 or 2, answer question 28 and skip questions 29, 30, and 31. If you checked response 3, skip questions 28, 30, and 31 and answer question 29. If you checked response 4, skip questions 28, 29, and 31 and answer question 30. If you checked response 5, skip questions 28, 29, and 30 and answer question 31.

28. If you checked response 1 or 2 to question 27:
    A. What are the specific criteria you look at in relation to the social worker's initial involvement in a case?

    _____
    _____
    _____
    _____
    _____

    B. What are the specific criteria you look at in relation to the diagnosis or assessment?

    _____
    _____
    _____
    _____
    _____

    C. What are the specific criteria you look at in relation to the goal-formulation or treatment plan?

    _____
    _____
    _____
    _____
    _____

    D. What are the specific criteria you look at in relation to the actual treatment or intervention?

    _____
    _____
    _____
    _____
    _____

    E. What are the specific criteria you look at in relation to termination, outcome, or follow-up?

    _____
    _____
    _____
    _____
    _____

29. If you checked response 3 to question 27, how do you measure client outcome?

_____

_____

_____

_____

30. If you checked response 4 to question 27:
    A. Have you developed a system for classifying clients' problems?
       1. ☐   2. ☐
          Yes   No
       If yes, attach a copy.
    B. Have you developed a system for classifying services or interventions by workers?
       1. ☐   2. ☐
          Yes   No
       If yes, attach a copy.
    C. Have you developed an instrument or procedure for measuring client outcomes?
       1. ☐   2. ☐
          Yes   No
       If yes, please attach a copy.

31. If you checked response 4 to question 27, have you developed an instrument to measure clients' satisfaction?
       1. ☐   2. ☐
          Yes   No
    If yes, please attach a copy.

32. Have you tested any parts of your system for validity and/or reliability?
       1. ☐   2. ☐
          Yes   No
    If yes, please describe your findings or attach a copy if available.

_____

_____

_____

_____

33. Have you developed a list of diagnoses or situations that indicate the need for social work assessments?
       1. ☐   2. ☐
          Yes   No

If yes:
  A. Please list these diagnoses or situations. _____

  _____
  _____
  _____
  _____
  _____

  B. Is this list used in the concurrent review activities of
     your hospital to identify cases in which a social
     worker referral should be made?
                    1. ☐   2. ☐
                       Yes   No
  C. Is this list primarily based on the following:
     1. Medical problems   ☐
     2. Psychosocial problems   ☐
     3. Other (Please specify.)   ☐
  _____

Analysis and Use

The questions in this section pertain to what is done with the information after it is collected.

34. How is your data compiled and analyzed?
          1. Informal, qualitative analysis   ☐
          2. Manual compilation   ☐
          3. Electronic data processing   ☐
          4. All the above   ☐
          5. No procedures for analysis   ☐
  A. If electronic, how did you obtain software?
          1. A program was specially developed for
             this system.   ☐
          2. An existing program was used. Please
             specify the name of the package from
             which it came.   ☐
  _____

35. What kinds of questions are answered by your analysis?
  _____
  _____
  _____
  _____
  _____
  _____

81

36. Are those answers useful for the following: (Check all that apply.)
    a. Management decisions ☐
    b. Improving practice ☐
    c. Evaluating the worker's performance ☐
    d. Other (Please specify.) ☐

    _____

37. Who receives reports of the findings: (Check all that apply.)
    a. All social work staff ☐
    b. The workers whose cases were reviewed ☐
    c. The worker's supervisor ☐
    d. Hospital administration ☐
    e. Hospital utilization review ☐
    f. Hospital PSRO committees ☐
    g. Regional PSRO groups ☐
    h. Others (Please specify.) ☐

    _____

38. What action has been taken in the department as a result of the findings? (Check all that apply.)
    a. In-service training ☐
    b. Continuing education ☐
    c. Personnel action ☐
    d. Administrative changes ☐
    e. Policy changes ☐
    f. Advocacy ☐
    g. Further research ☐
    h. Other (Please specify.) ☐

    _____

39. What has been the impact of your system on the following:
    A. The worker's performance:
       1. ☐   2. ☐   3. ☐
       Negative   No   Positive
       change   change   change
    If change observed, please describe and give evidence.

    _____
    _____
    _____
    _____

B. Client outcomes:
   1. ☐   2. ☐   3. ☐
   Negative   No   Positive
   change   change   change
If change observed, please describe and give evidence.

_____

_____

_____

_____

C. Departmental costs:
   1. ☐   2. ☐   3. ☐
   Increase   No change   Decrease
If change observed, please describe and give evidence.

_____

_____

_____

_____

D. Image of social work department in hospital and community:
   1. ☐   2. ☐   3. ☐
   Negative   No   Positive
   change   change   change
If change observed, please describe and give evidence.

_____

_____

_____

_____

E. Social work recording:
   1. ☐   2. ☐   3. ☐
   Negative   No   Positive
   change   change   change
If change observed, please describe and give evidence.

_____

_____

_____

_____

Please do not forget to attach copies of forms.

APPENDIX B

Quality Assurance Programs Studied

Programs Examined

Informants

1. *Quality Assurance System*, Department of Social Work, City of Memphis Hospital, Memphis, Tenn.

Frank Boatwright, Director, Department of Social Work, City of Memphis Hospital, Memphis, Tenn. 38103

2. *Social Work Audit and Peer Review*, Stamford Hospital, Stamford, Conn.

Mona Stone, Director, Social Work Department, Stamford Hospital, Shelburne and West Broad Street, Stamford, Conn. 06902

3. *New England Social Work Regional Program*, Massachusetts Chapters of Society of Hospital Social Work Directors, National Association of Social Workers and Academy of Psychiatric Social Workers, Boston, Mass.

Barbara Berkman, Lecturer, School of Social Work, Simmons College, 51 Commonwealth Avenue, Boston, Mass. 02116

Golda Edinburg, Director, Social Services, McLean Hospital, 115 Mill Street, Belmont, Mass. 02178

J. Frederick Glynn, Chief, Social Work Services, Veterans Administration Hospital, Brockton, Mass. 02401

4. *Peer Review System*, Social Service Department, Massachusetts General Hospital, Boston, Mass.

Eleanor Clark, Director, Social Work Services, Massachusetts General Hospital, Boston, Mass. 02114

5. *Quality and Quantity Assurance System*, Social Service Department, Mount Sinai Hospital, New York, N.Y.

Helen Rehr, Director, Social Service Department, Mount Sinai Medical Center, 11 East 100th Street, New York, N. Y. 10029

6. *Quality Assurance System*, University of Virginia Medical Center, Division of Social Work, Charlottesville, Va.

Miriam C. Birdwhistell, Director, Division of Social Work, University of Virginia Medical Center, Charlottesville, Va. 22901

7. *Quality Assurance Program,* Social Work Department, University of Michigan Hospital, Ann Arbor, Mich.

Kris Furgeson, Social Work Department, University of Michigan Hospital, Ann Arbor, Mich. 48109

8. *Connecticut Data Base,* Connecticut Chapter, National Association of Social Workers, Hartford, Conn.

Regina W. Falcon, School of Social Work, University of Connecticut, West Hartford, Conn. 06117

9. *Social Service Audit System,* Social Work Division, Strong Memorial Hospital, Rochester, N. Y.

Martin Nacman, Director, Social Work Division, Strong Memorial Hospital, 601 Elmwood Avenue, Rochester, N. Y. 14642

10. *Quality Assurance Program,* Social Work Department, Cincinnati General Hospital, Cincinnati, Ohio

Herbert Allen, Director, Social Service Department, Cincinnati General Hospital, 234 Goodman Street, Cincinnati, Ohio 45267

11. *Social Work Peer Review Program,* Texas Society for Hospital, Social Work Directors, Dallas, Tex.

Harriet Stambaugh, Director, Department of Social Work, Children's Medical Center, 1935 Amelia, Dallas, Tex. 75235

Family Ability to Meet Health Care Needs, Department of Social Work, Children's Medical Center, Dallas, Tex.

12. *One Adaptation of Social Work to a Peer Review System,* Medical Social Services, E. W. Sparrow Hospital, Lansing, Mich.

Mabel E. Meites, Director, Medical Social Service, E. W. Sparrow Hospital, 1215 East Michigan, Lansing, Mich. 48902

13. *Social Work Peer Review,* Department of Social Work, Johns Hopkins Hospital, Baltimore, Md.

Patricia Volland, Director, Department of Social Work, Johns Hopkins Hospital, Baltimore, Md. 21205

14. *Social Work Audit,* Department of Social Work, Hospital of University of Penna., Philadelphia, Pa.

Joan Bonner Conway, Director, Department of Social Work, Hospital of University of Pennsylvania, Philadelphia, Pa. 19096

15. *Social Service Review,* Beth Israel Hospital, Boston, Mass.

Betty Gumpertz, Director, Department of Social Work, Beth Israel Hospital, Boston, Mass. 02215

16. *Small Department Peer Review System,* Task Force on Small Department, Peer Review, Philadelphia area, Pa.

Lois Portnoff, Director, Social Work Department, Suburban General Hospital, Norristown, Pa. 19401

85

17. *Social Work Accountability Structure,* Social Service Department, University of Minnesota Hospital, Minneapolis, Minn.

Robert Spano, Director, Social Service Department, University of Minnesota Hospital, Box 181, Mayo Building, Minneapolis, Minn. 55455

18. *Professional Review Audit,* Department of Social Work Services, Long Island Jewish-Hillside Medical Center, New York, N. Y.

Abraham Lurie, Director, Department of Social Work Services, Long Island Jewish-Hillside Medical Center, New York, N. Y. 11004

19. *Social Work Audit,* Social Service Department, Cuyahoga County Hospital, Cleveland, Ohio

Janet Pray, Chairperson, Quality Assurance Committee, Cuyahoga County Hospital, Cleveland, Ohio 44109

20. *Audit-Peer Review,* Social Service Department, Cook County Hospital, Chicago, Ill.

Helen Jaffe, Director, Social Service Department, Cook County Hospital, 1825 West Harrison Street, Chicago, Ill. 60612

21. *Peer Review Program,* Department of Social Work, University of Maryland Hospital, Baltimore, Md.

Jean Dockhorn, Director, Department of Social Work, University of Maryland Hospital, 22 South Green Street, Baltimore, Md. 21201

22. *Self-Analysis Manual for Maternity and Infant Care,* Case Western Reserve University and Westinghouse Electric Corp., Cleveland, Ohio

Elizabeth Campbell, Director, Neighborhood and Social Services, Cleveland Maternal and Infant Project, 1803 Valentine Avenue, Cleveland, Ohio 44109

23. *Quality Assurance System,* Clinical Social Work Department, Denver Department of Health, Denver, Colo.

Jane Collins, Director, Clinical Social Work, Denver Department of Health and Hospitals, Denver, Colo. 80204

24. *Record Keeping System,* Social Service Department, Harborview Medical Center, Seattle, Wash.

Rona Levy, School of Social Work, University of Washington, Seattle, Wash. 98195

Karil Klingbeil, Director, Social Service Department, Harborview Medical Center, Seattle, Wash. 98104

25. *Criteria for Social Work Problem Oriented Record,* Social Service Department, Martin Luther King Hospital, Los Angeles, Calif.

Tessie Cleveland, Director, Social Service Department, Martin Luther King Hospital, 12021 South Wilmington Ave., Los Angeles, Calif. 90059

26. *Peer Review/Audit System,* Social Work Department, Richland Memorial Hospital, Columbia, S. C.

Jon G. Keith, Director, Social Work Department, Richland Memorial Hospital, 3301 Harden Street, Columbia, S. C. 29203

27. *Social Service Department, Internal Audit,* Social Service Department, Hillcrest Medical Center, Tulsa, Okla.

Melva Deakins, Director, Social Service Department, Hillcrest Medical Center, 1120 South Utica, Tulsa, Okla. 74104

APPENDIX C

Example of a Quality Assurance Program

This is a description of a fictitious quality assurance program. It is built from components of several of the programs examined and from findings about typical practices. It is presented here to illustrate the operations of a program.

The Social Work Department of Healthful Hospital, a six-hundred-bed teaching hospital with twenty-five social workers, has been involved in developing a quality assurance program since 1975. A committee of five social workers, with consultation from a medical records analyst and a systems analyst from the Data Processing Department, has been primarily responsible for developing the program. The department director has regular discussions about quality assurance with the hospital administrator, the chairperson of the hospital's PSRO committee, and other directors of social work departments in the area. Members of the local Society for Hospital Social Work Directors have worked together to develop some of the criteria now used at Healthful Hospital.

The quality assurance program has three components. The first is a patient-oriented information system that collects data on each patient and processes the information electronically. The actual data-collection form appears as Form A on pp. 90–91. One such form is completed for each social work patient. Monthly reports are produced from these data and focus on the following:

- The kinds of problems seen for each demographic group.
- The services received for each type of problem.

•Problem status at closing for each type of problem and service received.

•Problem status at closing for different demographic groups and types of problems.

•Resources used for each type of problem.

•Problem status at closing for each type of resource used.

•Means and standard deviations of number of contacts for types of services, for each type of problem, and for each worker.

•Special reports by request.

These reports are used in several ways. The quality assurance committee reviews them to see whether outcomes are acceptable in general and for specific types of patients. When outcomes are not acceptable, more detailed studies are undertaken or corrective action initiated. Findings that suggest patterns of practice are shared with staff through staff development programs; particularly important findings are written for publication. Supervisors and administrators use workload findings and practice patterns to guide some personnel and management decisions.

The second component of the social work quality assurance program is a peer review system. Through this system, a 5 percent random sample of closed cases is reviewed each month by a medical records analyst. She applies a set of criteria developed by the quality assurance committee and approved by the entire social work staff. Medical records are reviewed to see whether the social work process reflected therein is consistent with what is believed to be acceptable practice as reflected in the criteria. The format used is that recommended by JCAH, and a sample of the audit criteria used in this type of format appears on pp. 92–93 as Form B.

The first column of Form B contains elements that are important to examine in social work practice. When 100 percent appears in the second column, this element should always appear in the medical record. When 0 percent is specified, this element should never appear in the patient's record. The third column lists the legitimate exceptions to each criterion. The fourth column contains instructions to the reviewer.

When any of the cases examined fail to meet the criteria, these cases are reviewed by the committee. When it is determined that deficiencies exist, corrective action is initiated.

The director is also involved in planning a multidisciplinary study of kidney dialysis patients. These criteria for social work practice will probably be incorporated in that review.

Last year a report from the information system revealed that a large number of patients receiving the department's continued care planning services were achieving unacceptable outcomes. Therefore, the quality assurance committee decided to do a special study of patients in need of home care. These cases were randomly selected from a list produced by the information system. The results of this study appear on Form C, pp. 94–95. These findings resulted in some modification of departmental procedures. A follow-up study was planned to see whether the observed deficiencies were corrected. Other studies of this type are undertaken as problem areas become apparent through the information system or other sources.

The third component of the quality assurance program involves facilitating access to social work services. The committee has developed a list of indicators for social work services that have been circulated throughout the hospital (see Form D). A random sample of all hospital admissions is reviewed regularly to determine whether patients with these characteristics are actually receiving social work services. When gaps are found, corrective action is taken. For example, it was learned through such a review that many types of cases were not being referred from the walk-in clinic. All walk-in patients are now routinely screened by a social worker placed in that clinic. Efforts are under way to incorporate some of these criteria into the concurrent reviews now conducted by the medical records analyst.

Finally, a small random sample of social work patients is telephoned by clerical staff one month after case closure to determine their satisfaction with services. The interview schedule appears on Form E. The results of these follow-up interviews are submitted to the committee for review and possible corrective action.

The social work quality assurance program at Healthful Hospital is continually revised based on experience and new knowledge. It is also increasing its interface with the hospital's PSRO activities.

FORM A[a]

Unit Number
☐☐ ☐☐ ☐☐

Race
☐ 1. White 3. Puerto Rican ___
☐ 2. Negro 4. Other ___

Age
☐☐☐

Marital Status
☐ 1. Single   4. Widowed
   2. Married   5. Divorced
   3. Separated

1. Male
☐ 2. Female

Interpreter Needed
☐ 0. None   3. Deaf
   1. Spanish 4. Other ___
   2. Italian

Diagnostic Code
☐☐   Diagnosis ___

Social Worker ID
☐☐

Month
☐☐

Year
☐☐

Date Referred
☐☐ ☐☐

Referral Status
☐ 1. New
   2. Continued
   3. Reopened

Date Closed
☐☐ ☐☐

Transferred
☐☐ ☐☐

End of Month Status
☐ 1. Closed
   2. Continued
   3. Transferred

Posthospital Care Code
☐☐

PATIENT SERVICE SUMMARY

Billing Information
(Check one or more boxes.)

☐ Self
☐ Blue Cross/
   Blue Shield
☐ Medicare
☐ Medicaid
☐ Medicare/
   Medicaid
☐ University
☐ Compensation
☐ Other

Problem Typology (Check one or more.)

	Problem	Subcategory (Specify.)	Status of Problem at End of Month
☐	Interpersonal Conflict	___	☐
☐	Dissatisfaction in Social Relations	___	☐
☐	Problem with Formal Organizations	___	☐
☐	Difficulties in Role Performance	___	☐
☐	Problems of Social Transition	___	☐
☐	Reactive Emotional Distress	___	☐
☐	Inadequate Resources	___	☐
☐	Intrapersonal Conflict	___	☐
☐	Other ___	___	☐

Key:
1. Resolved
2. Decreasing
3. No change
4. Increasing

90

FORM A[a] *(Continued)*

Active Referred to Other Hospital and Community Services Primary Service Code Contact Person Telephone Inpatient Contacts Monthly Total

Social Work Services

Discharge/Planning/Coordination
Coordination/Referral/Conference with Community Services, Others
Coordination/Referral/Conference with Community Services, Others
Continued Care Planning/Coordination
Coordination/Referral/Conference with Community Services, Others
Coordination/Referral/Conferences with Hospital Services
Psychosocial Evaluation
Patient Psychosocial Treatment
Family Psychosocial Treatment
Group Psychosocial Treatment
Case Consultation
Advocacy
Other

Outpatient Contacts Monthly Total

Total

Location Hospital Service

Total

Location Hospital Service

[a] Form developed and used by Social Work Division, Strong Memorial Hospital (Program 9); reprinted with permission.

91

FORM B[a]

HOSPITAL:
Audit Committee: Social Services

Date: 9/15/77

Element	Standard 100% 0%	Exceptions	Instructions and Definitions
Documentation of a referral assessment	100%	**1** A. Patient left hospital within forty-eight hours of referral B. Routine team referral (stroke, spinal cord, burn, Neonatal Intensive Care Unit)	Look in social service report for evidence of information gathered about referral, such as (1) discussion with RNs or other staff members, (2) discussion with physicians, (3) review of medical records, (4) discussion with Admitting Department or Emergency Room, and (5) discussion with patient or family.
Acknowledgment by documentation within two working days	100%	**2** A. Death of patient within forty-eight hours of admission B. Referral arrived just prior to intervening weekend (after 12:00 noon Friday) C. Outpatient referral	Look for date of social service documentation on consultation sheet or social service report form.
Statement of problem related to hospitalization and care of the patient	100%	**3** A. Death of patient within forty-eight hours of referral B. Patient left against medical advice C. Social service referral declined	Look in social work notes for statement of referral problems, or indications for social services.

FORM B[a] (*Continued*)

Element	Standard 100%	0%		Exceptions	Instructions and Definitions
Subjective and objective data that verifies or validates problem statement	100%		4	Same as exceptions in Box 3	Look in social service report for assessment of problem.
Is there a statement of goals or plans or proposed actions by the patient or the social worker in behalf of the patient?			5	Same as exceptions in Box 3	Look in social service report for statement of plans. Look in case closings for units of service.
Record of action taken or services provided by the social worker	100%		6	Same as exceptions in Box 3	Look for record of action in program notes of social service report.
Documentation of the outcome to the identified problems	100%		7	Same as exceptions in Box 3	Look in social service report for statement of resolution of problem or look for statement of improvement of problem or problem outcomes.

[a] These criteria were developed by the Social Service Department, E. W. Sparrow Hospital, Lansing, Michigan (Program 12); reprinted with permission.

FORM C[a]

AUDIT TOPIC: PATIENTS IN NEED OF HOME HEALTH CARE

II. Data Display

A. Number of Records Reviewed 28   Number of Physicians in Study____   Committee: Social Service   Date:____

Physician Distribution:____   B. Number of Males____ Females____   Completed by____

Patient Age Distribution____

No.	C. Criteria	D. Actual Practice[b]		E. Comp. Not Meeting Management	F. Variation Charts		G. Distribution	H. Comments and Correlations
		No.	Percentage		Practice	Document		
1.	Consultation with ward personnel (physicians and/or nursing) concerning referral of patient apparently suitable for Home Health Care.	28	100					
2.	Interview with patient and/or family concerning description of Home Health Care and to secure consent for participation in program.	28	100					
3.	Visiting Nurse Association referral made and documented.	28	100					
	a. Signed physician's order sheet (including date of first clinic appointment).							
	b. Staff report sheet of supportive service activities which must include Social Service description of home situation.							
	c. Discharge planner sheet.							
4.	Securing of necessary prostheses, appliances, and sickroom supplies.	27	96					Family disappeared. Visiting Nurse Association could not visit.

Measurement | Variation Display

94

FORM C[a] (*Continued*)

No.	C. Criteria	D. Actual Practice[b] No.	D. Actual Practice[b] Percentage	E. Comp. Not Meeting Management	F. Variation Charts Practice	F. Variation Charts Document	G. Distribution	H. Comments and Correlations
5.	Arrangements for suitable transportation upon patient's discharge.	0	0					Transportation not documented.
6.	Observation of written nurse progress report within two weeks post-discharge, and regularly thereafter.	27	96					No progress report on family.
7.	Documentation of home visits by social worker if required by visiting nurse.	28	100					No social service visits appear necessary.
8.	Documentation of first clinic visit following discharge.	24	86					Four patients refused clinic follow-up.
9.	Transfer of social service information to outpatient.	24	86					No record of transfer (see No. 8).
10.	Documentation of multidisciplinary case conferences as indicated.	28	100					
11.	Documentation of ongoing Social Service coordinator involvement.	28	100					
12.	Readmission to hospital on priority basis if advised by visiting nurse.	28	100					

FORM D[a]

Universal Indicators

Explanation: The following represents a list of recommended indicators to define all patients in the health care system who should automatically be referred to the Department of Social Work Services:

1. Any patient admitted from a nursing home, chronic care facility, or foster home.

2. Any patient whose condition will affect his or her ability to return home.

3. Any patient with no known family or adequate social and financial support system.

4. Any patient with a history of frequent readmission or hospitalization within one year.

5. Any patient exhibiting prolonged fear and/or anxiety about recommended medical procedures.

6. Any patient who is a suspected victim of abuse, neglect, or violence.

7. Any patient with identified problems whose medical compliance hinges on adequate housing and/or physical conditions.

8. Any patient whose condition will necessitate a change in education, employment, and/or family roles.

9. Any patient whose condition has resulted in identified problems that will negatively affect self-image, appearance, and physical and/or sexual functioning.

10. Any patient whose identified family problems directly affect care, treatment, and compliance with medical recommendations.

11. Any patient or patient's family exhibiting behavior that is disruptive to treatment.

12. Any patient who is a nonresident of this state and has an illness that will affect his or her ability to return home.

13. Any patient admitted for treatment as a result of a catastrophic event.

14. Any patient in the terminal stages of illness.

15. Any patient whose hospitalization and/or medical compliance depends on specific concrete supports in the home.

---

[a] This form is part of a list developed by the Social Work Department, Johns Hopkins Hospital (Program 13); reprinted with permission.

FORM E[a]

Social worker assigned to patient _____

Individual doing interview _____ ‚

Interview for month of _____

Primary Client Follow-up Telephone Interview

Check one:

Name _____   Call completed _____

Address _____   Cannot find _____

Telephone _____   Refusal _____

                                 Deferred _____

Relationship to patient (If primary client is the patient, check.) _____

Is patient deceased? Yes____ No____

Check type of patient: Clinic____ Hospital____

Check the answer that best tells the interviewee's opinion:

1. I saw the social worker as soon as I wanted or needed to.   Yes____No____Do not know____

2. I saw the social worker as much as I wanted or needed to.   Yes____No____Do not know____

3. The social worker understood what I wanted or needed.   Yes____No____Do not know____

4. The social worker explained how he or she would help me.   Yes____No____Do not know____

5. The social worker seemed concerned about me.   Yes____No____Do not know____

6. My contact with the social worker helped me better understand and deal with my concern or problem.   Yes____No____Do not know____

7. I knew how to contact the social worker if I needed to.   Yes____No____Do not know____

8. The social worker was thorough and organized in his or her efforts to help me.   Yes____No____Do not know____

9. More patients should take advantage of the services of the Social Work Department.   Yes____No____Do not know____

10. Social workers at the hospital could improve their services to patients and families.   Yes____No____Do not know____

Comments from patient/family about any of the questions _____

_____

_____

_____

Check degree of validity as determined by the interviewer:

Poor____   Fair____   Good____

[a] Form developed by the Social Service Department, City of Memphis Hospital (Program 1); reprinted with permission.

97

APPENDIX D

Example of a Detailed Problem List[a]

FAMILY RELATIONSHIP

21 Family situational problem.
22 Chaotic, disorganized, or dysfunctional family system; multiple psychosocial and environmental crises.
23 Conflicts in family system.
24 Change in expected dependence-independence roles—for example, overidentification of opposite sexual role, child assuming adult social roles within family, or illness and hospitalization causing adult shift in roles.
25 Children at risk for neglect, abuse (physical or sexual), maternal deprivation, inadequate performance of role as parent, or lacking parental skills.
26 Voluntary or involuntary absence of family member causing individual or family upset or dysfunction.
27 Conflict between couple.
28 Any other problem in family relationships not previously described.

LIVING CONDITIONS

310 Lack of housing.
No shelter available on discharge or imminent loss of shelter.

---

[a] From Department of Social Work, Johns Hopkins Hospital (Program 13); reprinted with permission.

311 Substandard conditions.
Physically deteriorated housing adversely affecting health.
312 Need for supports in the home: helping agent or equipment required for the maintenance of the patient in the community.
313 Questionable institutional arrangements with likelihood of placement.
314 Long-term placement in chronic nursing home.
315 Short-term placement, usually involving rehabilitation and period of convalescence.
316 Caretaker in the home not able to provide adequate care; abusive or neglectful guardians.
317 Other.

INDIVIDUAL OR FAMILY FUNCTIONING
RELATED TO ILLNESS

318 Time, understanding, or intervention necessary to adapt to lifestyle changes as a result of illness.
320 Not keeping appointments, taking prescribed medication, or following prescribed treatment or other medical recommendations.
321 Actions or behaviors are disruptive; staff expectations not clearly communicated.
322 Individual or family refuses prescribed treatment procedure.
323 Individual or family do not understand the nature of the illness or its potential effect on lifestyle.
324 Taking unusually long and possibly harmful length of time in deciding to accept or reject recommended treatment.
325 Vague complaints are not symptomatic of any documental physical problem; they are, rather, clues to minor emotional or social distresses.
326 Real symptoms could be associated with specific disease, but are not validated by physical work-up. Person firmly convinced of disease and believes it has an organic basis.
327 Time, understanding, or intervention necessary to adapt to changes in lifestyle brought about by terminal condition.

328 Condition is stable and requires permanent change in lifestyle. It may require permanent dependence on others.

329 Any illness-related social or emotional dysfunction not previously described.

DIFFICULTIES IN INTERPERSONAL RELATIONSHIPS

330 Voluntary or involuntary absence of meaningful social contacts.

331 Difficulties sustaining satisfying relationships with members of age group.

332 Problems in coping with school routines, underachievement, or learning disorders.

333 Problems in coping with work routines or underachievement.

334 Delinquency, running away, incorrigibility, or chronic truancy that is apart from school adjustment or performance problems.

335 Disobedience, destructiveness, temper tantrums, lying, physical and verbal aggressiveness, or hostile teasing.

336 Child abuse, chronic physical fighting, wife beating, repeated disruptive arguments, and hostility.

337 Sexual deviations or difficulties in sexual performance.

340–344 Temporary financial crisis

345–347 Medical insurance coverage

OTHER SPECIAL CONDITIONS

350 Estate planning problems.

351 Legal problems.

352 Educational planning problems.

LACK OF KNOWLEDGE OF COMMUNITY RESOURCES

353 How to utilize resources.

354 Eligibility for resources.

355 Other.

BEHAVIORAL SYMPTOMATOLOGY

410 Alcoholism.

421 Drug addiction or dependence.

412 Hyperkinetic.

413 Bowel and bladder control problems without organic cause.

414 Stuttering, aphasia, or the like.

415 Under- or overeating that affects health and relationships; eating nonedibles.

416 Personality disorders including sociopathy.

417 Obsessive compulsive behavior that interferes with functioning.

418 Physical symptoms caused by emotional factors (psychophysiologic disorders, hysterical conversion, compensation neurosis).

419 Acute reactions without underlying mental disorder, usually called "adjustment" reactions, such as in response to unwanted pregnancy, enforced retirement, school failure, or birth of sibling.

THOUGHT OR MOOD DISTURBANCES

430 Temporary depression in reaction to a situation that is generally recognized as warranting a feeling of sadness.

431 Excessive or lasting depression with or without a precipitant.

432 Chronic depression that is long-standing, but usually with fluctuating intensity (often associated with low self-esteem or early cultural and emotional deprivation).

433 Manic depressive illness.

434 Situations in which the risk of suicide or manipulation through threats of suicide are the central problem, with or without depressive illness.

435 Temporary anxiety in reaction to a situation that is generally recognized as warranting apprehension.

436 Excessive or lasting anxiety with or without a precipitant.

437 Phobias or excessive fear reactions.

438 Chronic or borderline schizophrenia.

439　Acute psychosis characterized by such symptoms as hallucinations, delusions, gross distortion of capacity to meet ordinary demands of life or to perceive reality. The psychosis may be temporary or permanent, and it may be associated with schizophrenia, drug or alcohol poisoning, or physical trauma or illness.

440　Organic brain syndromes without psychosis.

441　Mental retardation.

2M/79
2M/9/80